"'The Essential Guide To Mystery Shopping' is the best book on mystery shopping to come along in years! I couldn't put it down once I started reading! After seven years as a mystery shopper, I found myself nodding my head in agreement at the suggestions. It's a must have for mystery shoppers."
Paula Kutka, Mystery Shopper, Houston, TX

"I have known Pam for as long as I have been shopping. Whenever in need of advice, I have turned to her as she has been through everything and anything that can happen to a shopper! Years of experience combined with the heart of a teacher have led her to share her knowledge in 'The Essential Guide to Mystery Shopping.' It should be required reading for every Mystery Shopper!"
Servanne Edlund, Full-Time Shopper, Silver Lake, MN

"Pam knows thoroughly the ins-and-outs of the mystery shopping trade; from locating the most stable and best-paying companies, to the most effective ways to communicate with mystery shopping firms, and to identifying and utilizing the tools and skills that are of most benefit to both seasoned and novice mystery shoppers. This is an ever-changing business and there is always something new to learn; this book is truly essential."
Nora Simon, Mystery Shopper, Philadelphia, PA

"Regardless of my 10 years of full time experience, telling friends and family how to get into mystery shopping was no easy task. No matter what, it was so overwhelming for them, to the point of giving up. PamInCa wrote this book with meticulous fashion and detail that a clueless breakout mystery shopper would feel guided in the right direction."
Josh N, Florida

"A well-researched guide on mystery shopping, complete with a list of reputable companies, has been long overdue. Pam has written the ultimate book, providing helpful information to anyone who has considered mystery shopping as a career or as extra income. Both experienced and new shoppers will benefit from the organized and detailed information. Pam is considered one of the most professional and experienced evaluators in the country; this book could not be written by a more qualified researcher."
Judy Camus, MSPA Shopper of the Year, 2007, Virginia

"Many companies seek first-hand insights about what customers experience inside their restaurants, hotels and stores, and this successful mystery shopper known by the pen name PamInCa tells it like it is. If you're curious about what it takes to become an undercover shopper, read her book. PamInCa's informed and practical insights can help you to become a retail sleuth who's in demand."
Michele Chandler, Assistant Communications Director
Stanford Graduate School of Business
and former Retail Business reporter
San Jose Mercury News

"This book is a must-have for anyone wishing to pursue mystery shopping. It has all of the information necessary to get started. Wish I had this ten years ago when I was starting out!"
Judy Poole, Independent Contractor
and Business Owner
Former Educator and US Navy Veteran

"I met Pam on a message board and found a really nice person that has a lot of knowledge about mystery shopping. She has helped me find jobs and she has helped me learn how to enter the reports. I am very grateful to Pam. She really cares about people and helping them with this kind of work. I have never met anyone that would go out of their way to help you make money. Thank you so much Pam."
Mary Smith, Full-time Mystery Shopper

The Essential Guide to Mystery Shopping

PamInCa

HappyAb☺ut.info

20660 Stevens Creek Blvd., Suite 210
Cupertino, CA 95014

Copyright © 2009 by PamInCa

First Printing: June 15, 2009
Paperback ISBN: 978-1-60005-130-2 (1-60005-130-8)
Place of Publication: Silicon Valley, California USA
Paperback Library of Congress Number: 2009930277

eBook ISBN: 978-1-60005-131-9 (1-60005-131-6)

Trademarks

Warning and Disclaimer

A Message from Happy About®

Thank you for your purchase of this Happy About book. It is available online at http://www.happyabout.info/mystery-shopping.php or at other online and physical bookstores.

- Please contact us for quantity discounts at sales@happyabout.info
- If you want to be informed by e-mail of upcoming Happy About® books, please e-mail bookupdate@happyabout.info

Happy About is interested in you if you are an author who would like to submit a non-fiction book proposal or a corporation that would like to have a book written for you. Please contact us by e-mail editorial@happyabout.info or phone (1-408-257-3000).

Other Happy About books available include:

- 42 Rules for Working Moms
  http://happyabout.info/42rules/workingmoms.php
- Lessons About Life Momma Never Taught Us
  http://happyabout.info/lessons-about-life.php?PHPSESSID=8ad846
  e8778212396581f8ae962e4492
- Confessions of a Resilient Entrepreneur
  http://www.happyabout.info/confessions-entrepreneur.php
- Memoirs of the Money Lady
  http://www.happyabout.info/memoirs-money-lady.php
- Happy About Extra Hour Every Day
  http://happyabout.info/an-extra-hour.php
- Happy About Working to Stay Young
  http://www.happyabout.info/working-to-stay-young.php
- Forever Free From Chronic Pain
  http://happyabout.info/nopain.php
- Care: You Have the Power!
  http://happyabout.info/care.php
- 42 Rules for Saving Your House
  http://www.happyabout.info/42rules/savingyourhouse.php
- Wealthy U: Seven Sacred Wealth & Wisdom Lessons
  http://happyabout.info/wealthyu.php

Dedication

To Ray Sola: Owner of Volition.com, LLC. For his Web site, for countless hours of hard work, and for what he offers shoppers across the world for free. His personal interactions with me have helped me to become a better communicator.

To Lorri (Kern) Hsu: Owner of KSS International, Inc. For her devotion to this business, and for being my mentor. I respect her deeply and appreciate all she has done for me and for others in this business.

To my family: For being so patient.

Acknowledgments

There are so many people who have contributed to this book that I would require another chapter to thank each one. So even though they are not all listed here, I am extremely grateful to all of them. I appreciate the support and contributions from the many shoppers, companies, and friends that have helped me. Among them there are some people who have made a big difference in the last year. To them I extend my special thanks.

To Ray Sola, who came up with the great title of this book and offered his support and guidance throughout my adventure.

To Paula Kutka, Servanne Edlund, Nora Simon, Carrie Kern, Kim Gilbert, Josh Northrup, Michele Shepard, Jana De Anda, Jenny Miracle Turner, Michael Linck, Judy Poole, Michele Chandler, Deb Riker, Anne Harris, Aileen Mullee, Heather Sandifer, Mary Smith, Marlene Wilson, and all of my Volition.com friends.

A special thank you to Larry Olmstead, who helped me locate a publisher who would listen.

To Tony and Teneyah Olmstead for accompanying me on jobs that required their time and energy, and for little or no pay for research for this book.

A note to those who stay home to help children grow

My daughter is now sixteen. She has been mystery shopping with me since she was eight years old. She knows what good service is and how customers are supposed to be treated. She knows how to behave in all types of situations from receiving the wrong food at a fast food location to walking into a five-star restaurant. She has an excellent memory now and will always be the one who can describe what the person who robbed the bank looked like.

She now does compliance jobs and enjoys the extra money it pays her. She says she will do this all through college. She has not started doing her own reports yet as the companies require an adult to do that, but as soon as she is of eligible age, I will pass that onto her as well.

Mystery shopping provided me with the opportunity to be home, pick her up from school, and be around during those peak hours (3 pm to 6 pm) when kids get into trouble. When she is doing her homework, I work on my reports. Thus, she doesn't feel she is the only one having to sit quietly and work.

She gets all As and Bs; she was elected into ASB, the student government at school; and she is taking college credits with advanced classes in high school.

Although I do not take credit for her great performance, I believe that if I had continued my full-time career, her school years would have been different and she would have suffered without the additional support I've been able to give her.

She will be eighteen in a year and a half and off to college. I will miss my shopping buddy! So, all of you who are doing this so you can be there with your kids, trust me, it will pay off. You will always be glad you did it. Parents and grandparents are and always have been the best teachers.

Contents

When my youngest daughter was born, I decided to work from home. So I became a data entry specialist and started processing mail-in rebates for a local company. Unfortunately, the workload was sporadic and the task repetitive. Moreover, the skimpy paychecks didn't allow us to go out much and our budget was quite tight. In order to bring the fun and excitement back into our family routine, I needed to find a way to make a few extra dollars that would not be dedicated strictly to paying bills.

I recalled that when I was working in a restaurant we had mystery shoppers come in and evaluate the service they received. I looked up the Internet for information on mystery shopping. As I tried to decipher the incredible amount of information available, I came across a multitude of scams and other unrelated Web sites. It took quite a bit of patience and dedication to distinguish between what was real and what was just too good to be true. More than once I felt like giving up. However, I am not a quitter and I don't like starting something and not finishing it. I was determined to get to the bottom of this mystery shopping phenomenon.

After a few unsuccessful searches, I found Volition. com©. This was an invaluable source of information for the beginner that I was. But it was difficult to understand the language these people used. I didn't know what most of them were talking about.

All along, as I was negotiating the long learning curve, I kept thinking I didn't really know what I was getting into. A new surprise revealed itself every day, making it harder and more discouraging than the day that had gone by.

It seemed like a lonely business run by independent contractors who don't get to talk to their office buddies about the day's misadventures. One would never know if others had had the same experience. I have second-guessed my decisions more than once when faced with an unusual situation, as I had no idea whether I was doing the right thing. If only I had been able to reference one trusted source of information on the spot, it would have put my fears at ease.

The Essential Guide to Mystery Shopping provides that much needed, trusted source of information I was so desperately looking for in my early shopping days. In this book, you will find answers to the most common questions. The mystery shopping lingo has been translated into English and everything you absolutely need to know before getting started is here. With this book in hand, you can start your successful career as a mystery shopper with a positive mind-set as you will know exactly what you are getting into. There is no need to wonder indefinitely whether you've done the right thing or not. The answers to your questions are most likely here. Congratulations, you have finally found your inseparable mystery shopping companion in *The Essential Guide to Mystery Shopping*!

Happy shopping!

Servanne Edlund
BSc (Business and International Law)
Université de Rennes I—Law School, France

Introduction[1]

Eight years ago while browsing the Internet I found a site called Feedback Plus. It said they did mystery shopping. I had no idea what this was so I did a search, which led me to a number of scam sites that said: "Pay $29.95 and you'll get paid to eat and shop." "Make $20.00+ an hour." I checked out a few of the links on the search page and returned to the home site. I looked carefully through all the information; there was no mention of any fees to work for this company. I thought to myself (as I filled out their application): "There must be other companies out there that do this." However, I was working full time and my search for the "urban legend" of mystery shopping was half-hearted. I received an e-mail reply from Feedback Plus stating they didn't need anyone in my area at the time, so I just let it go and didn't think about it any more.

Many months later, as I was sitting at the computer looking over my favorites file and enjoying a glass of wine, I again noticed the Feedback Plus site. I decided to do another search. Of course, technology progressing like it does, this time I discovered a lot more information which led me to a mystery shopping forum. I was stunned at the

---

1. The author wants to remain anonymous and will use her pen name PamInCa.

number of people actually doing this work. It was legitimate, it was not a myth. Most importantly, they were not paying to mystery shop. This is where it all began.

I signed up with companies and applied for various jobs. I quickly became addicted and quit my office job to become a full-time mystery shopper. I worked seven days a week for eight years, the latter half of which was spent on research for this book. I have completed mystery shopping jobs of all types, and many of which I would never do again based on their requirements and pay. Sometimes I ended up making less than a dollar an hour. But you will reap the rewards of my efforts.

None of the companies listed here charge a fee to work for them. Mystery shopping is not an urban legend. It is real; you can eat and shop and get paid for it. Mystery shopping has evolved into a worldwide business. With an uncertain economy, companies are desperate to keep their customers—and they need you! This is not the best-paying job in the world, but whether you want to do it full time or supplement your income part time, or if you just want to have a free dinner at an expensive restaurant, my book will help you navigate your way through a maze of information.

I created this book to teach new shoppers how to get started—the process can be overwhelming. It will also benefit the experienced shopper by offering new tips on reporting and possibly even list new companies for you to consider working for. It will lead you, the new shopper, to these companies, tell you what types of jobs they offer, how to apply, how to successfully complete the job, and how to write the reports. My goal was to write a book that would prevent you from making the same mistakes I made. There are things that can only be learned through years of experience in this business. I am pleased to share these valuable tips with you in this guide.

1 What Is Mystery Shopping?

Mystery shopping is a tool used by companies to measure the quality of service, food, and the overall experience of the everyday customer. The concept behind mystery shopping is not new. Kings were known to disguise themselves as commoners and mingle with common people to find out what was being said about them and their kingdom. How many times have you wished you could be a fly on the wall?

Mystery shopping as we know it today seems to have begun in the 1940s as a way to measure employee integrity. In 1941, the first mystery shopper appeared in the movie *The Devil and Miss Jones*. A shopper approaches Jean Arthur and Charles Coburn, who are working behind a counter in a department store. She makes her purchase and, following the transaction, reveals her identity and demands that Coburn stop chewing his gum! Integrity shopping is still done but now the business has ventured into many other areas. Although some revealed shops such as the one in the example above exist, the majority are covert, and the activity is performed secretively.

The consumer demand for better service has seen a constant growth for some years. Companies struggle to meet this demand due to high employee turnover, shrinking profit margins, and increasing competition. At the same time, owning and maintaining a successful business has become more complex and difficult with the almighty Internet offering 24-hour shopping with no waiting lines, products delivered directly to consumer's homes, and many sellers to choose from. Efficient, friendly service is now a basic consumer expectation.

Mystery shopping is among the most powerful tools available to companies seeking to improve their service quality and offer speedy service at the same time. Providing objective data about service execution across a broad range of locations and delivery channels allows managers and company owners to identify specific areas that need improvement, and to reward employees in a consistent, relevant manner. The need for this research will only increase as customer demand for high-quality, efficient service grows. With today's current economy, businesses cannot afford to lose customers. Thus, as competition in businesses is growing, so is the need for mystery shopping.

Virtually every company has some type of mystery shopping program in place. Few are done internally; most companies prefer the anonymity offered by mystery shoppers as well as the ability to check on hundreds of locations in a short span of time. In an industry with more than 1.6 million US retail establishments, including departments, specialties, discounts, catalogs, the Internet, independent stores, chain restaurants, drug stores, and grocery stores, it is easy to see why mystery shopping has become a much sought-after service.

Although mystery shopping started in the 1940s with retail establishments, today it has expanded to hotels, casinos, theme parks, after-school care, assisted living facilities, cruise lines, banks, and more. Not all mystery shopping needs to be done in person; there are phone and online jobs as well.

As consumers, our time is valuable no matter what type of service we are in need of. We don't have the time to be on hold for ten minutes; nor do we want to order a product online and be promised a two-day delivery, which ends up taking a week. Mystery shopping does and will continue to change the way businesses train their employees to offer consumers satisfactory services and keep having them come back. Be a part of that change, starting today.

Mystery shoppers are common people who visit a variety of business locations and report back on the service, food, ambiance, cleanliness, timings, and the overall level of customer service. They make observations based on the particular requests of each client and they are required to enter this information on a form. Generally, this is done over the Internet, but on occasion it may be done manually and faxed, e-mailed, or mailed to the company they are working with. Mystery shoppers have a keen eye and great memory, or at least they possess great note-taking abilities. They are astute, honest, and are able to provide facts without including their opinions. They are moms, dads, professionals, educators, CEOs, college students, and teenagers. They are compensated for their time and effort with fees paid for each job or offered a reimbursement for their required food or purchase. It is not uncommon to receive both.

2 What Tools Do I Need?

You will need different tools as your mystery shopping business grows. For starters: a computer, printer, transportation, and pens and paper are enough to get you well on your way. A digital camera is useful, but it's possible to work without one. There are a few companies such as DSG© that allow shoppers to work without having a computer, but such companies are quickly becoming extinct.

Some things will never change. You will always need to keep a positive outlook and be willing to work with schedulers and companies. You have to be dependable and you need to take this work seriously. There are too many shoppers out there who don't follow through, so please don't be like that! Let's go over some of the tools listed above.

Pens: It's best not to use red or bright colors as these will be more easily noticed than black or blue. Scribble on your notepad first to see how they look. If it gets your attention, it will most likely get other people's attention as well.

Notepads: Good ones to use are Oxford® View Front Ruled Index card spiral.

Sample note card:

Store /location	Time in _____	Time out _____
Info	Info	Info
Info	Info	Info
Info	Info	Info

Computer: You don't need a high-tech computer. As long as you can connect to the Internet you can do mystery shopping. If you don't have a computer, use the one at your local library.

Printer: You will need to use your printer almost daily. I have found it best to buy an "All in One" printer which will allow you to scan receipts, make copies, and print. If you are buying a new printer for this work, check the cost of the ink refills before making the purchase. You will need a lot of ink so you should buy a printer that uses lower-priced ink.

Digital camera: Many jobs will require photos. You can buy a digital camera for around $60.00 these days. It does not have to be fancy; the less fancy, the easier it is to hide in your pocket or purse while taking discreet photos. This is one item for which it's well worth the money to purchase the extended warranty from the store.

As you can see, you can start with very little and have a successful career in this field.

3 Getting Organized

Before applying to any company you need to have your answers to the questions in this chapter. It is essential to organize your thoughts and recognize your personal needs and wants from this job in order to be successful and happy with this work.

Q. How much time do I have? How much time do I want to invest doing this?

If you work full time and have small children at home, you obviously have limited time. If you are single and work forty hours a week, but have nothing else to do, you have more time to spare. Make sure you are realistic with the time you HAVE to do the work and the time you WANT to spend doing the work. There can be a huge difference in what you want and what you have. Don't overload yourself, everyone will suffer and you will not like doing this job any longer.

Q. What days and hours can I work?

Get a calendar and keep it beside your computer. Ensure you enter all scheduled activities. This includes the time you go to work and leave, the time you drop off your kids, etc. Every job you accept or are assigned will have specific days and sometimes specific hours during which it has to be completed. Of all the assets, the calendar is one of your most important ones. If you are computer savvy, keep a record of this information online. But, and this is a big but, do not rely solely on your online calendar. Technology is wonderful when it works, but it doesn't always work. Always have a hard copy!

Q. What types of places do I like to visit?

The answer to this question will be just as unique as everyone who is reading this book. Everyone has places they love to visit. For some it's apartments and new homes, for others it will be the mall. For me, it's the grocery store. Remember, there is nothing that does not get shopped. Having a list of what types of places you want to visit will help you when you're looking for jobs. Visiting places you like to visit will help make this transition into mystery shopping easier and more fun. In the beginning, being familiar with the types of places you are visiting will make it easier to look for, and report back on, particular client requests. I highly recommend only visiting places you like for the first few weeks to get a feel for mystery shopping and what is expected of you.

Q. What types of places do I dislike visiting?

You are probably thinking there is no place you wouldn't visit if the money is right. This can be a big mistake. If you hate going to the mall or movies, then you already have a preconceived opinion regarding these locations. This can affect your ability to give an objective report. There are lots of jobs out there and there is no need to visit places you don't like to go to as a consumer. For most, this list will be small. Not going to one or two types of places won't be detrimental to your success as a mystery shopper.

Q. What would I like to learn about?

Perhaps you want to buy a new car, home, or electronic device. What better way to do your research than getting paid for it? Every imaginable type of business is mystery shopped. Keep a list of what you want to learn about and watch out for these jobs.

Q. Am I doing this for fun or to make money or both?

Determining your reason for doing this job is important. If you need to make good money quickly, do not take reimbursement jobs or jobs that require you to spend money to make money. There will be more about those types of jobs in Chapter 5. If you want to eat out more often and not affect your current budget, then look for those types of jobs. Whatever it is you are doing this work for, be realistic and honest with yourself upfront so you're not spinning your wheels, wasting time applying to companies that don't offer the types of jobs you want.

Q. How much money do I want to make?

This question goes hand in hand with the previous one. Determine how much you need to add to your current income or budget and write this amount down. Each time you add a new job, write down how much it pays so you can hit your monthly total. Make sure to keep track of pay and reimbursements separately.

Q. What impact will this job have on my family?

If you have a family and are responsible for dinners, homework, etc., make sure to take jobs that will still allow for that time. Remember to add reporting times to the jobs you take. You will find the estimated reporting times for various jobs in Chapter 5. This job can have positive and negative effects on your family based on your organization. Again, do not overload yourself. I cannot stress this point enough!

Q. How much time do I want to spend on reporting?

We are all different and the amount of reporting we like to do will be as varied as the jobs we decide to take. If you like to focus on one thing for long periods of time, take jobs investigating apartments, fine dining, and hotels. If you like to move quickly and get onto the next thing, take jobs in areas such as grocery, gas stations and fast food.

Q. Am I a good writer?

Be honest with yourself. If you aren't, you will be setting yourself up for extreme frustration. If you struggle with spelling and grammar, don't take jobs that will require long narratives. There are plenty of companies such as TrendSource, Market Force, and Corporate Research that require minimal narratives. You don't need to be a stellar writer to do this job.

Now you are ready to move on to the next steps. Let's go through them to help you create your new mystery shopping image.

Take note of my pen name, PamInCa. This was created when I visited my first mystery shopping forum and is now what everyone in the mystery shopping circles knows me as. Think of something that has your name in it, and something that will sound professional and easy to remember. You will also be using this name for mystery shopping forums so you can visit them and chat with other shoppers. Volition.com requires all registrants to use part of their real name. Write down several ideas and then go to http://www.yahoo.com, http://www.hotmail.com, or http://www.gmail.com, or you can use the same company you have your current personal e-mail address with.

You need to create an e-mail account exclusively for your mystery shopping business. Yahoo offers free e-mail to everyone; I've found it to be one of the easiest to work with. AOL seems to have many issues with mystery shopping companies; it thinks their e-mails are spam because of the number of e-mails they send out. You can have more than one e-mail account, so signing up with Yahoo or any other e-mail will not affect your existing e-mail accounts. If the name you have chosen is not available, it will show you alternatives. If you like one—great; if not, enter one of the other names you have written down. Continue doing this until you have found something that suits you. Pick a password; it should be easy to remember. Once you have your name and password chosen, write it down in this space.

You need to keep track of every username and password you create or that is created for you by mystery shopping companies and forums. With over 400 mystery shopping companies, this can become very confusing, very fast. Once you apply for a company and have a username and password, write it in the space next to the company information in this book. This will help you tremendously. The same goes for the forums you visit too.

Once you have your new e-mail and user name (example: PamInCa), you are ready to register at http://www.volition.com. This will be your portal to meet, chat, and get to know other mystery shoppers. Try to always have a positive attitude when relating to shoppers on the forum. Remember, this is a business and you should conduct yourself in the same professional manner you would in an office setting. You do not have to post on the forum, but if and when you choose to do so, post only after you have carefully read what you have written, checking for spelling and grammar errors. Make sure what you write makes sense and fits the thread (online conversation) that is being discussed. Remember, companies and schedulers also read this forum, so sell a positive image of yourself while remaining honest at all times. Remember two important things: You should never ask which mystery shopping company shops a particular client and you should never tell which mystery shopping company shops a particular client.

Applying to Companies

Before applying to any company, you still have one more step to go. You will have to prepare certain items in advance. Open a word document on your computer so you can type this information. Copy and paste it into the mystery shopping companies' application forms. If you do not know how to create and open a word document, now is the time to learn. On my computer, if I right click in the middle of my computer screen, I see the word "new." When I put my mouse over this, it offers: folder, shortcut, briefcase, and "Microsoft Word Document." Click on "Microsoft Word Document" and it will save it to your desktop. You can then double left click and a blank page will appear. At the top left corner of your page you will see "Save as." Give this page a title, something along the lines of "Mystery shopping company info." Make sure you save it to your documents or any location that is easy for you to find. Look at the box that appears in the middle of your screen to see where it's being saved. You can click on that box to change the location. Write this down here.

Now open this document by double clicking on the icon. Type this information into the document and then make sure to save it again. This information is non-negotiable in most cases. The companies need to make sure you are a legitimate person before sending you out.

Full name

Address

Birth date

Social security number

Phone number

Areas you want to shop. Do this by city and zip code. I have found that http://www.zip-codes.com© is one of the easiest to use.

Sample Narrative

Most companies will want some type of narrative about a recent dining or retail experience. This does not need to be long but it must state the facts and not opinions. Your narrative should consist of 200–500 words, but not longer unless the company specifically requests a longer one.

Read the samples provided to get your thought processes working, but do not copy the samples to use as your own. There are more detailed narratives later in the book, but this will give you a good idea of what you need for now.

Sample Restaurant Narrative

As I approached the location, I found it to be clean and nicely maintained. The windows and doors were washed and there was no debris visible. The cash area was clean and the baklava case and drink cooler were free from dirt and well stocked. The tables and chairs were spotless and there was no visible debris on the floor. The tables were cleaned within a few seconds of guests leaving. The drink station was fully stocked, but there were splatters on the back splash and the counter top. The restroom was clean and fully stocked.

I was greeted as soon as I entered the restaurant. The cashier was polite and efficient. He offered assistance during my ordering process and recommended the combination plate, a better deal than ordering each item individually. My food was delivered quickly. It was excellent, served fresh and hot, and was very appealing to the eyes as well as to the palate.

The team worked well together and the service was phenomenal. Each team member I interacted with smiled, made eye contact, and greeted me in a friendly manner. I was very impressed with the service I received. Overall, the visit was terrific and I would highly recommend this location based on today's visit.

Sample Retail Narrative

As I neared the location, I found the exterior to be well kept and free of debris. I opened the door and found the glass at the entry and the front windows clean. I entered the store and the associate at the front register smiled and said hello. The carts and baskets were at the front and easily accessible to customers.

As I browsed the store I found the aisles orderly and all items neatly arranged and clearly priced. The store had a wonderful variety of merchandise; shopping there was enjoyable because of the cleanliness and organized layout, the clear, signage and the attractive placement of products on the shelves.

I approached the register and found that no one was in line. Christine looked at me, smiled, and asked if I had found what I was looking for. I said yes. She rang up my items and asked if I was a Rewards member. I handed her my card and she processed my transaction quickly and correctly. She handed me my receipt, smiled, thanked me, and wished me a good day.

4 Planning My Month

This is probably one of the hardest things to do in this business. It becomes very easy to over-schedule yourself no matter how long you have been mystery shopping. When you are first starting out, I do not recommend scheduling more than one or two jobs a day. You will need to focus and give yourself ample time to read the instructions, print the forms, and prepare yourself mentally for completing the job and entering the report. You should allow yourself at least as much time to enter the report as it takes you to complete the job. I also do not recommend taking too many of the same type of assignments until you do at least one and see if you like it or not. There's nothing worse than scheduling eight bank jobs to find out, after the first one, that you'd rather have all of your teeth pulled out than do this kind of job again!

Always have a calendar with any events for the current and upcoming month in front of you. Make a copy to keep in your car, in case a scheduler calls you to complete a job. You need to know what you have planned and what city you will be in every day of the month.

Fill in your calendar with anything you have to do: work, appointments, kid's schedules, events, etc. as soon as you know the dates. This way, when accepting an assignment, you can quickly see if you're going to be available to do the job within the required time frame. When you accept an assignment, immediately put that in your calendar along with specific times of the day, if required. Note the city as well so you can schedule other jobs for that area on the same day. Once you have scheduled a job in a particular area, scour the self-assign jobs and add other jobs to your schedule. Add jobs that are en route to and fro. Don't worry if you cannot find another one right away. Jobs are posted daily and most likely at least one will be posted in the city you're visiting.

When you see one of the larger companies such as CoRI, TrendSource, Market Force, or Service Intelligence, post their jobs; note it on your calendar. You will quickly see a trend. A lot of companies post around the same time of the month, every month, and some have certain days they post the majority of their jobs on. I have been successfully able to schedule jobs around the days or times of the month that I know other jobs from companies will be posting. I know that most companies post on Mondays and Fridays, so I try to ensure I'm home in the mornings or watch the computer more closely on those days.

Write in pencil. You will find there will be jobs you can and need to move around to different days or time periods. Writing in ink can make your calendar difficult to read. However, if you have a job that has a strict time frame and must be completed on a certain day at a certain time, use a red pen. This way each time you look at your calendar, you will see it bright and bold to help you remember.

You will also see many companies post jobs the month prior to the actual job due dates. This is an added benefit and will help you make more money if you start selecting these jobs early. So fill the days in with job offers from schedulers and self-assign sites in the same areas. It makes no sense to drive ten miles for ten dollars when you can add a gas station or quick drive-through lunch to the trip.

You can add dates on your cell phone or Google calendar to send you reminders of visits. Although there are many fancy ways to organize your monthly calendar, I always seem to go back to printing two from the PrintFree© Web site. It offers me a simple sheet of paper to carry and be able to reproduce quickly if I need to. Once I complete an assignment, I use my pencil to lightly mark through each job. You may want to be able to see that job at a later date to keep track of payments, so don't make it too difficult for yourself.

I rarely schedule important events or vacations on the first and last weeks of the month. Most jobs will post during the first and last weeks, as well as bonused shops posting in the last week. Until you have a firm understanding of when companies are posting, and how to take jobs while traveling, try to leave these weeks free for your mystery shopping jobs. Throw away or destroy your calendar after six months, unless you have infinite storage space. In a year's time, you will accumulate more paper, receipts, brochures, flyers, and business cards than you know what to do with. You can also scan each completed month's calendar and save it to your computer. Trust me, try to minimize the amount of paper you save in any way you can.

5 Questions and Answers

New shoppers inevitably ask the same questions. Finding jobs and knowing how to complete them can be difficult at best when first starting out. This chapter will cover the most frequently asked questions and I have answered them for you with as much accuracy and honesty as possible.

Finding Jobs

Q. Who shops "such and such?"

This is the most common question. When you register with a company, you sign an Independent Contractor Agreement (ICA). Read this carefully. Every company has their own version, but they basically say the same thing. Anyone working as an independent contractor for a mystery shopping company should honor the ICA. Don't share client information, forms, etc. Don't ask who shops Ted's Market; shoppers will not be able to tell you and they will most likely be annoyed that you asked them.

Q. How do I find shops in my area?

Shoppers always ask how to find jobs in their area. Please do not ask shoppers on mystery shopping forums who has jobs in your area. This is ever-changing as clients move from one company to another. There is no easy answer to this, but it helps to make sure you have great communication with schedulers and are willing to travel. Look outside the box. If you see a job 50, 100, or more miles from you, start searching for jobs with other companies and see if you can self-assign other jobs that would make it worthwhile. Most of the time, if a job is paid highly for a city, it means that city is not shopped often. Thus, many companies will have jobs that are bonused in the same city. If I make $1.00 per mile driven, then I feel I've been fairly compensated. This is generally not as successful by working for just one company. The following is an example of an actual route I could take at the time this was written.

Corporate Research (CoRI) has a gas station that is 300 miles from my home and it will take me over four hours to get there. One job is paying $65.00. I broaden my search and find that there are three other gas stations on the same main road en route to this location that are paying $65.00 each. So, I am at $260.00. I check the other self-assign companies to find one drive-through at a fast food location paying $55.00 for a drive-through lunch, plus reimbursement; another one a few miles down the same main street in the same small town is offering $51.00 plus reimbursement for a breakfast. I also found two more companies with jobs in the same area paying between $25.00 and $50.00.

Now I have a good base. I am at $418.00 with eight jobs I can self-assign from four companies. But I am not going to self-assign yet. I know these jobs are difficult to schedule, so I call the companies and make my offers. I ask for $10.00 over and above what is offered on the job boards of all four companies. You can always ask for more, but I am suggesting $10.00 to simplify the example. So eight jobs with an additional $10.00 each puts me at $498.00.

Remember, my goal is $1.00 per mile driven. The round trip is 600 miles. While I am on the phone with each company, I ask if they have other jobs in the area that need completing. Each and every company has at least one job to be done in the area and offers a fair price, $25.00 for most. I hit my goal.

I schedule these jobs, and then continue with my search. I e-mail the schedulers I regularly work for and let them know my travel locations and dates. I receive two offers. One job is paying $35.00 and the other $75.00. None of these jobs will take more than twenty minutes each to complete and the reports will take even less.

I am well over my goal, but now I decide I might want to spend the night at the first city as it's the furthest away and drive back home the next day. I have two choices: look for a hotel shop or stay at the local hotel I found for $45.00 a night. As looking for hotel shops can be time-consuming, I choose to stay at a hotel I find without doing the additional work. My friend Servanne, who shops all over, would have chosen the hotel shop. Many shoppers do not mind driving the eight or ten hours it will take to make the trip. The bottom line is if there is no work in your area, look outside the box; in this case, outside of your area. Most of my time is going to be spent driving. I can pick up books on tape at the library, listen to my favorite music, or even plan a family getaway.

Oftentimes shoppers will do a 100-mile or more radius search so they can plan a route. By doing the larger radius search, it will also show you what types of jobs a particular company has that may not be available to you at the present time, as someone else has already picked them up for that particular month. Make note of any of these jobs and the company you see them with, and watch for them to post for the following month.

Look at the mystery shopping boards and read them a little differently. Actively search for posters that live in the same area as you do. If they are posting on threads relating to TrendSource or another company you are not registered with, register with that company. When looking at the job boards, search for your state, not just for your city, and apply to those companies.

You can search sites like Yahoo and Google for mystery shopping in your state at http://groups.yahoo.com/group/XX-MysteryShops. For example, if your state is Tennessee, you type in http://groups.yahoo.com/group/TN-MysteryShops.

Use caution, though; carefully read what you find. Remember, you should not have to pay any company to work for them. It is unnecessary unless you really don't have the time or desire to apply to the companies listed in this book and on the mystery shopping forums. If you decide you want to use a service, it appears that many shoppers have used Shadow Shopper with good results. To use this service, type in this Web site address: http://www.shadowshopper.com/?adid = 4014. There are no others I would recommend at this time.

Even if you find a company you think sounds great, search for feedback on the company on http://Volition.com. I do not recommend shopping for any company you cannot find feedback on. You risk spending your own money and time without ever getting paid or, worse, reimbursed. Sign up with the scheduling companies listed in Appendix C. They will offer a large variety of jobs with many businesses. This is one of the best ways to see the largest number of companies with shops in your area. Remember, scheduling companies do not pay you, they simply assist mystery shopping companies in finding shoppers for jobs they need completed. Most of the scheduling companies will help you if you run into a payment problem, but there is no guarantee this will happen.

Make sure you are signed up with every company that offers "Self-Assigning." I have not found any of these companies not having jobs in every state. You will know they are self-assign companies as an (S) appears next to their name in the company directory (Appendix C).

If there is a restaurant, store, or other facility in your area and you want to know who does their mystery shopping, call them or their corporate offices and ask. Many times they will be glad to tell you. If they say they are not mystery shopped, contact one of your favorite companies and let them know. They will probably be very interested in contacting them and might even offer a referral fee for your information.

Q. When are jobs posted?

Most companies start posting jobs during the last week of the month through the first week of the following month. However, CoRI and TrendSource are two companies, among others, who post throughout the month, so keep checking the job boards, particularly for the self-assign companies.

Q. Is there a list of legitimate places to apply with?

Volition.com and the MSPA list companies that are legitimate.[2] There are several other companies that are legitimate but not listed on these Web sites, including the ones mentioned in Appendix C. If you have great success with a company and it is not listed on Volition, make sure to share it with the owner of Volition.com via e-mail. Always search for feedback on any company you are considering working for before accepting a job. You

---

2. Although these sites list companies they know to be legitimate, we are not responsible for changes made by the individual companies. Company changes and feedback from shoppers are vital to the continued success of these forums.

can search for feedback on both Volition.com and the MSPA Web site. Chances are extremely high someone has worked for them in the past. If you cannot find any information on the company, post a question on one of these two forums, making sure to list the company name and providing the link to the company's Web site.

Q. Where do I find the mystery shopping forums and how do I sign up for them?

I recommend signing up at Volition.com first before taking any assignments and reading as much as you can. Signing up is free and although you have to wait to be approved by the moderator, it is a relatively short period of time. You are welcome to read prior to registering, but you cannot post onto the forum until you have been approved. I also recommend signing up at the MSPA forum. Both links are given below. Make sure to read all of the rules prior to signing up. Do not skim through them, read them carefully!

Volition.com: http://forum.volition.com/

MSPA.org: http://www.mysteryshop.org/shoppers/forum/

Q. Can I apply for and accept jobs which were not offered to me?

Yes, as long as a job indicates availability, you can request it or self-assign yourself to it.

Q. How many companies should I apply to? How many am I allowed to apply to at the same time?

You should apply to several companies. Applying to one hundred or more companies is not uncommon. Not all will have work in your area all of the time, so you need lots of options. You are allowed to apply to as many companies as you deem fit and you can apply to all of them in a single day, if you choose. There is no limit to how many you can work for, even on the same day. You are an independent contractor, meaning your business is yours to run as it best suits you and your needs.

Q. How many jobs can I self-assign in one month?

This is completely up to you. However, some companies limit the number of jobs they'll allow a new shopper to sign up for. Service Intelligence and CoRI start shoppers off with fifteen jobs. You can request more, but you cannot self-assign more than this to start with. Service Intelligence will increase your monthly job allowance once you have worked with them for a while if you contact Support through their Web site. CoRI allows you fifteen open jobs at any given time, with the exception of their gas station jobs, which you can self-assign up to sixty at one time each month.

Q. How many jobs can I do in one day?

Some companies limit the number of jobs that can be completed for them or one of the clients or meal times in one day. However, the number of jobs you can complete for more than one company is up to you. You can schedule as many jobs with as many companies as you want in one day's time. Just remember some companies will require reporting on the same day. Try not to over-schedule yourself.

Q. Can my spouse and I both complete shops for the same company?

Most companies will allow more than one household member to work for them. Just make sure each of you does your own work.

Q. Can I take jobs in other cities while traveling?

Yes, note reporting times and make sure you will be able to enter the reports within the correct time frames. You can also e-mail companies and schedulers to let them know you are traveling to see if there is work available. Some companies are willing to extend due dates or the reporting time frames if you make arrangements in advance.

Q. I received an e-mail for a job offer in which the company sent me a $2,500.00 check. All I have to do is cash it, send $2,000.00 back, and I keep $500.00. Is this a legitimate job offer?

No, this is a scam. No legitimate mystery shopping company will ever ask you to cash any check for them. The only check you will ever receive from a legitimate mystery shopping company is for your completed work.

Self-Assigning and Applying for Jobs

Q. What is the difference between self-assigning and applying for jobs?

Self-assigning means you are automatically assigned and responsible for that job. Applying means several shoppers are applying for that same job, and you have to be accepted for it before you become responsible for that particular job.

Q. Once I accept a job, how long do I have to complete it?

All jobs will show you a due date. The date ranges are normally within a week. However, this varies by company. Read the due date before applying or self-assigning a job to make sure you will be able to complete it. You do not want to cancel jobs or reschedule jobs unless it is an emergency.

Q. Can I accept an assignment if the due date has passed?

No, you should contact the scheduler and ask if there are available dates for that particular job. Otherwise, you risk doing the job and not being paid.

Q. Can I complete a mystery shopping job for a company I work for at another location?

No, you should never complete a job for any company you, a friend, or family member currently work for. Most ICAs will clearly state this. Some companies require you not to have or know anyone that has worked for the client for the last five years.

Q. What does it mean when it says the start date is January 1st and the completion or due date is January 12th? Can the job be completed on January 2nd?

This simply means you can do the job on any date between the given dates. However, the job must be completed and reported by January 12th.

Q. Do I have to print documents as soon as I accept an assignment or can I do that later?

It's a good idea to print any necessary forms immediately and put them into a folder. They will be there until the assignment is completed and reported. If you want a copy for yourself, make sure to print the forms before submitting the report as it most likely will not be available after being submitted. Remember to consider the cost of printing these forms when accepting a job, as some jobs have ten to thirty pages to print and the job may not be profitable in the end. So only print what is necessary and save the rest in a file on your computer.

Types of Jobs

Q. What is a revealed job?

You will perform the job and, and once it's complete, reveal yourself to the client as a mystery shopper.

Q. What is a purchase and return job?

This means you must make two visits to the same location. Keep this in mind when you see the payment for these jobs. You will make a purchase and return it on two separate trips. You will need the information from both receipts. Take a photo or write down all the information from the purchase receipt before making the return.

Q. Are there any telephone shops?

Several companies offer phone shops: Market Force, TNS, Franchise Compliance, TrendSource, CoRI, Service Intelligence, Ace and Business Evaluation Services, to name a few. You will find them as you go along with your mystery shopping; most of the time they are sent to you from schedulers through an e-mail. However, some companies offer phone jobs and do not post them on their job board. After you have successfully completed work for different companies and shown your dependability, it does not hurt to ask the schedulers if they have phone jobs available.

Q. What are video jobs?

These jobs require the use of hidden cameras, most often supplied by the mystery shopping company. Shoppers have to secretly videotape their visit to a particular location.

Q. What is a compliance job?

This involves testing the associate to see if they are following the guidelines set either by law or by the company they work for.

Q. What is an integrity job?

This involves paying cash for an item to ensure the associates are ringing up the sales department and putting the money in the cash register.

Q. What types of jobs are available?

Just about every type of business you can imagine is mystery shopped. The most common are grocery stores, gas stations, fine dining, fast food, hotels, casinos, office supply stores, hardware stores, and convenience stores. More uncommon, but still shopped, are cruise lines, funeral homes, and even churches.

What Do I Need?

Q. Do I need a phone?

No, you can complete most mystery shopping jobs without a phone. However, you should invest in at least a home phone so schedulers can contact you with job offers. All companies will ask for a phone number on the applications, so if you do not have a home phone or cell phone, give your work number or a close relative's or friend's number, provided, of course, they don't mind.

Q. Are there any specific computer requirements needed to mystery shop?

No, as long as you can get online you can apply, accept, and complete mystery shopping jobs. However, if you are using a dial-up option, your system will run much slower. Also, using Internet Explorer seems to work best with most companies' reporting systems.

Q. What if I don't have a fax, scanner, copier, or printer?

Fax machines are quickly becoming antiques. Very few companies still use these. However, there is a Web site called Efax® that allows you to do this online. The link is provided in Appendix B. For scanning, copying, and printing, you can go to an office supply store and use their equipment, but I would suggest spending about $50.00 to buy an all-in-one machine. This will scan, copy, and print all your receipts and forms.

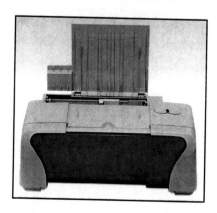

Q. Is a driver's license mandatory?

No, you can do work for most companies without a driver's license.

Reporting Jobs and Feedback

Q. How do I submit my shop results?

When you accept a shop or are accepted by a company to visit a shop, make sure to add it to your calendar. Write the company name, due date, and any information pertinent to that particular job in one place; this permits easy access both for reviewing the materials and, most important, for finding the company Web site to enter your results. Also, remember to take full advantage of your mail folders. All new jobs can go into a mail folder with "New Jobs" as the title. Once completed, move that job into the "Completed Jobs—not paid" folder; once paid, move that job into the "Completed jobs—paid" folder. Some shoppers keep everything on a spreadsheet. I've found it easiest to keep them right in my mailbox so that I have easy access whenever I am checking my e-mail from any device or location. (Note: If you use Cox as your e-mail provider, set up new folders. If you use Gmail, set up labels, which is the same thing as folders.)

Q. How do I know how many characters I can use for my narrative?

Some companies will clearly show on the report how many characters are allowed. But some don't and this can be a real pain if you have typed a 1000-word narrative to find, after you hit "submit," you are only allowed 500 characters. This can be like starting the report from scratch. If you remember to do **all** of your narratives in a word document, you will be able to count characters and remove or add them as needed.

Q. What is the best way to write my overall narrative?

Start from the beginning and work your way to the end of the visit.

Q. Do I have to explain all of the "yes" answers?

Not usually. However, some companies will want comments for all questions. This will be easy by following the tip above. All you have to do is copy and paste from your word document.

Q. What if I have completed many jobs for the same company and mixed up the reports by entering the information for one in place of the other, and submitted the wrong report for one of the jobs?

Contact the company immediately, own up to your mistake, and ask for help. They can put the report back into the system so you can enter it correctly. To avoid this, when entering your reports, separate them and look carefully at each job before starting your reporting. Keep only the information for the job you are working on in front of you. If you ever enter the wrong information for any job and have submitted that report, contact the company immediately.

Q. Do all companies give feedback on my reports?

No, most of the companies which use the SASSIE reporting software will offer feedback, along with a grade from 1 to 10. Others will only contact you when there is a need for clarification.

Job Requirements

Q. Can I bring someone (e.g. children) with me?

This will vary with job and company. Read the job details carefully before applying for or self-assigning any job.

Q. What if I forgot to get a receipt?

You will most likely need to redo the job. Contact the scheduler or company, own up your mistake, and ask for instruction. I have on occasion had companies allowing me to send a copy of my online bank transactions showing the location and amount spent.

Q. What if there is no receipt available due to something that is not in my control?

If there is a computer malfunction at the location you are shopping or the receipt gets damaged, try to get the associate to reprint the receipt if possible or have them handwrite the receipt, explaining you need it for your boss or some such reason. Some companies will tell you to ask only once for a receipt; if one is not offered, do not to ask again. Remember, reading all of your paperwork and having the notes for each job with you will help you to be successful.

Q. What if I visit a location that is closed?

Try to get a picture verifying the address or a picture of the closed location. When you enter the report, enter the job as closed. If this is not possible, contact the company or scheduler and ask for instructions. Generally, companies will pay a portion of the fees for all closed locations once it has been verified.

Q. What if it's the weekend and I need to cancel or reschedule a job due to an emergency?

Ninety-nine percent of the companies have some type of system in place for contacting them over the weekend. If you cannot find information on their Web site or in the e-mail from the scheduler, check Volition.com for help.

Q. What if I paid with a credit card and found out I was supposed to pay with cash only?

You will most likely have to redo the job. Contact the scheduler, own up your mistake, and ask for instructions.

Q. What if the client I am shopping will not take my credit card unless I spend a certain amount?

Always have enough cash to make your small purchase. Ask for a receipt and, if questioned, tell the associate you keep track of all expenses.

Q. What if I am supposed to purchase an item and the item is not available?

Generally speaking, you should purchase an item close to the original item, staying within the reimbursement allowed. For example, if you are supposed to purchase a hot dog and the grill is out of order, purchase a bag of chips or another small item. Report exactly what took place and why you could not purchase the required item. Always make some type of purchase so you will have a receipt as proof of your visit.

Q. Is it absolutely necessary to stick to the script given by the mystery shopping company or can I ad lib ask other questions or engage in small talk as well?

Generally speaking, you should make the conversation flow and not be canned in your questions and responses. This means do what comes naturally, ask questions, and get interested in your scenario so it seems more realistic. There are times when a company will require you to follow an exact script. This will be noted in your job instructions. In this case, do not change anything in the script.

Q. Do I need to record these extra things and include them in my report?

No, you can state that the associate made small talk and was personable. Report what the company asks for; there is no need to give details about your entire conversation.

Q. What if I cannot find an employee to assist me and the job requires an interaction?

Most job instructions will offer details as to what to do if this happens. I have seen the following instructions. Go to another department and ask for assistance. Ask a cashier for assistance, wait twenty minutes and leave the department, and explain what happened in your report. If the job states you must have an interaction, then you must, or your job will not be accepted and you will not be paid.

Q. Do I always need to make a purchase?

No, there are jobs such as banks, apartments, business verifications, car dealerships, phone shops, and more that do not require any out-of-pocket expense. However, they will still require a business card, a photo of the front of the store or another type of proof that you were at the location. Check your instructions. If you are not sure, contact the scheduler immediately.

Q. What do I do if I need to make a purchase and the store doesn't have anything that I need or want to purchase?

Don't take the job. Or purchase something for a gift for an upcoming event.

Q. How and when do I need to provide a receipt to the company?

The majority of companies will ask you to upload your receipt on their Web site as you enter the report. Some require the receipt immediately, others within twelve to twenty-four hours. Review your instructions for every job. Very few companies ask you to send the receipts. However, I know that some still require this. Make sure to save a copy of the receipts before mailing them. Some companies, such as Service Intelligence, will not require a receipt for every job. Check your job details. All companies will require you to hold onto your receipts for six months in case they need proof of your visit at a later date.

Q. The instructions state to get the first and last name of the employee but I was only able to get the first name. Is it really mandatory to get the last name as well?

It depends on the job and the company. You need to make every effort to get the last name if it is required. If you cannot, explain somewhere in your report the steps you took to get the last name and why you were not able to do so.

Pay and Reimbursement

Q. What is the difference between reimbursement and pay?

Reimbursement is the money you are required to spend to complete the job; pay is for your time filling out the report. You will get both if both are displayed in the job offer.

Reimbursements will be given to you in addition to the pay you are receiving for that job. You are required to spend your own money first and the company will reimburse you for the expenditure.

For example:

Payment $7.00

Reimbursement $12.00

This means you will be paid $7.00 for your time and reimbursed up to $12.00 for the required purchase.

Q. Can I buy items in addition to my required purchase?

This will vary from one job to another. For grocery stores, retail stores, etc., yes, this is perfectly fine. When you are completing a restaurant or fast food job, there may be specific items that you can order, with no additional items allowed. Remember that if you do purchase additional items, you will be reimbursed only the amount promised by the company for the required items.

Q. Do I get to keep the items I purchase?

Generally yes, unless you are doing a purchase and return shop, or if the company specifically states they want the merchandise returned to their office.

Q. How do I get paid if I don't have a checking account?

You won't. You need to set up a checking or savings account as all companies will pay you either by PayPal© or check. Many shoppers set up a bank account exclusively for their mystery shopping business.

Q. What is PayPal© and how do I set up an account with them?

Paypal© is an eBay© owned company that allows individuals and businesses to send and receive money online. The money can then be transferred to your bank account or, if you choose, to a PayPal© debit card.

To set up the account, go to https://www.paypal.com/ and click on "sign up" at the top of the page. Remember to use the e-mail address that is reserved specifically for your mystery shopping business. Sign up for the personal account and as long as you live in the United States there will be no fees incurred by you to add or withdraw funds, unless the mystery shopping company pays by credit card, which is rare.

Another feature is an optional PayPal security key. There is a one-time fee of $5.00 to add this to your account, but it will protect your identity and avoid money theft. Visit their security center for information on protecting your account. Never click on a link sent to you by e-mail from PayPal requesting you to log in and change information. E-mail them directly through their Web site or call them at 888-221-1161 or 402-935-2050.

Q. What additional out-of-pocket expenses should I expect to have?

As an independent contractor, you are responsible for all of your own expenses. This includes, but is not limited to, gas, paper, ink, Internet fees, postage, wear and tear on your car, and phone charges.

Q. How do I set up direct deposit?

All banks and credit unions offer this service. Call your banking institution. For all the companies that offer direct deposit, you will need to give them your account number and routing number. There is generally a section at each company's Web site telling you how to fill out the forms for the direct deposit. Routing numbers are generally the first group of numbers located on the bottom of your checks. Your bank account numbers are the second group of numbers. These are always separated by some type of symbols. Example:

Routing number	Account number
:; 123215978;:	.;125786485123:;:

Q. What is a 1099?

This is a form sent to independent contractors for work completed for specific companies. It is used for non-employees. A copy will be sent to you, another to the IRS, and one will be kept on file at the company you completed the work for. You will receive this if you earn $600.00 or more from any one company. Some companies will mail 1099 forms to everyone who has contracted with them throughout the year.

Q. How do I make a profit?

Take a variety of jobs. Take jobs that offer reimbursements for items you need to purchase; bundle jobs when you can. Take jobs that require no out-of-pocket expense, such as apartments, bank jobs, or cell phone jobs. Check the IRS Web site for deductions allowed on your new small business.

Notes and Timings

Q. How do I remember everything?

You need to take very good notes. Prior to completing any job, write down all the questions on your notepad. The majority of the time the questions will be similar: date, time in, time out, associate name, description, waiting time, etc. Simplify this process by using the Oxford Spiral notebook and write the name of the location you are visiting at the top. Chapter 7 gives an example of how this can be done. Some shoppers use a DVR; personally, I find listening to this while trying to enter reports difficult.

Q. How can I take my timings and not be seen?

Use a small notepad and visit a restroom, use your cell phone to keep track of timings, use a non-sounding stopwatch, keep a small crossword puzzle or newspaper within your reach to act as if you are involved in another activity. Be creative.

Who/What Is This?

Q. What is Volition.com?

Volition is the largest mystery shopping forum in the world. Shoppers in many countries use this free forum to find jobs, to connect with other shoppers, and to get advice. Be sure to check out all areas of Volition.com.

Q. What is JobSlinger.com?

JobSlinger.com is a search engine for finding jobs. However, the jobs shown on this site are also available on Volition.com.

Q. What are Sassie, Prophet, Client Smart, Mystery Shop Solutions, and ShopMetrics?

They are reporting systems used by mystery shopping companies to allow shoppers and schedulers to view, assign, and report jobs. They are not mystery shopping companies and do not pay shoppers.

Q. What are scheduling companies?

They are scheduling services used by mystery shopping companies to reach a broad range of shoppers. They are not mystery shopping companies and do not pay shoppers.

Q. What is the MSPA?

The Mystery Shopping Providers Association is an organization for companies. They provide shoppers with certification courses that can increase their ability to acquire jobs with companies who recognize certification and prefer to use certified shoppers. For more information, go to http://www.mysteryshop.org/shoppers/ and read all the information available to see if you feel it would assist you. I have been Gold Certified since 2003 and it has opened many doors for me. But many shoppers report having plenty of work even without the certification, so it is not mandatory.

Q. Should I get certified before applying for jobs?

If you have $15.00 you could complete the Silver certification, which will not hurt, but it is not required. My suggestion is to complete a few jobs and make sure this is something you want to pursue before spending any money on certification.

Q. What is the difference between an MSPA workshop and a conference?

The MSPA workshops are a one-day training course which provides shoppers with the Gold certification.

The MSPA conferences are larger; they have more company reps, generally last for three days, and provide an opportunity to network with a large number of shoppers. This information can be found by visiting the MSP link above.

Questions Regarding Privacy

Q. Does my name remain anonymous to the company when they see my report?

Your anonymity should be, and usually is, protected from the client's view. (It has been reported by other shoppers that EPMS gives your name to their clients.) The only other exception to this is a "Revealed" job.

Q. Do I have to give out my social security number?

No, not until you are actually working for a company. You can put 000-00-0000 or 111-22-3333 into the space requiring the number on the application. However, all companies do require a social security number or some type of tax ID number to pay you. You can apply for an Employer Identification Number (**EIN**). You may obtain this form by visiting the Internal Revenue Service Web site at www.irs.gov and download form SS-4 on the left side of the page. You can use this instead of your social security number for most companies. You can also call the company requesting the information and give your social security number over the phone, so it is not sent over the Internet. Remember, you want to search for feedback on these companies before giving out your personal information. Don't get excited and jump into anything—always use caution.

Q. Do the mystery shopping companies deduct taxes?

No, you are responsible for keeping track of all your earnings and paying the appropriate taxes if due.

I recommend John D. Brown, CPA, LLC, to complete your taxes. He is a mystery shopper as well as a CPA. He can be reached at 317-471-8505.

Q. Can I cancel a job that I have self-assigned or been scheduled for if I change my mind?

No! This will have an impact on your rating with the self-assign companies and schedulers may very well remove you from their database. Only cancel an assignment if it is an emergency situation.

Q. What if I decide mystery shopping is not for me? Do I need to contact any of the companies or do I just stop accepting assignments?

With the exception of Service Intelligence, which offers the subscription program, you can just stop self-assigning or accepting assignments. Please make sure to complete any assignments you have already accepted. E-mails will continue to be sent to you, but you can either delete them or keep your options open. You never know when something may come along that sounds interesting to you. For Service Intelligence, you will need to log into their system and cancel any active subscriptions. If you need help, e-mail their help desk through the link on the front page at the top left.

What Does This Mean?

There are a variety of terms used by mystery shopping companies that you will need to become accustomed to. Some are simple and need no explanation. However, when it comes to reading questions on your mystery shopping forms, you need to know exactly what the company is looking for, not what you think they are looking for.

If you run across a mystery shopping form that has a word you are unfamiliar with, and that is not listed in Appendix A, contact the company right away and get an explanation. This is yet another reason to read the documents and instructions as soon as you are assigned a job, whether it is self-assigned or assigned by a scheduler. Add the new word and its explanation to the list in Appendix A, so you will have it handy the next time.

If you get the job over the weekend or cannot get a response in time, go to Volition, search the mystery shopping forum for feedback on that particular company and post your question there. Someone will, without fail, know the answer. And, unlike most mystery shopping companies, the shoppers at Volition are open 24 hours a day.

6 Narratives and Word Documents

I have included narrative samples at the end of this chapter. Some are simple and some are much more complex comprising 2000 or more words. Some reports will take you less than five minutes to complete. Others can take more than six to eight hours. You are welcome to use them as samples to lead you through your reports, but never copy them exactly. You need to make every visit unique and each report should reflect that unique visit.

With that said, you will find that you do the same type of report again and again. Write and save **all** your narratives in a word document or word-processing program. This will help minimize grammar and spelling issues by utilizing the spell check offered in these programs. It will also offer you a saved report to refer to, so that you avoid making copies when completing narratives you will be writing in the future. If you do twenty bank reports for the same company each month, you will know after the first one is graded what the company expects. All companies will require unique reports regarding each job, but some things will always remain the same. Here is an example for a bank report:

Was the exterior clean?

The exterior was clean and well maintained.

Note: Using the term "well" should be limited. If you have used it more than twice in a single report, use another term in its place, such as nicely maintained, or use the word maintained, with no qualifying word in front of it.

Was the ATM clean and were customer supplies stocked?

The ATM was free of debris and the supplies were fully stocked.

Grammar/Spelling/Narrative Tips

I am by no means an English scholar and being a mystery shopper has really taught me how little I know about the use of the English language. Here are some tips I have picked up from editors over the years.

Write all narratives, no matter how big or small, in a word document or word-processing form to minimize small spelling and grammar issues. Spell out your numbers, such as ten, twenty, and thirty, not 10, 20, 30.

Do not write in CAPS only.

Do not use the same words as those used in the question. Come up with specific, descriptive words to communicate what took place during your visit. However, if the question uses a specific term to describe the employee, such as associate or team member, repeat this term when writing your narrative.

Do not use qualifiers such as very, somewhat, extremely, really, etc. Pick the appropriate descriptive word and leave the qualifier out of the sentence.

Do not include any reference to previous visits.

Refrain from using or including unconstructive terms or comments of personal preference (e.g. never, finally, simply, should/could have). The company doesn't care if you prefer low fat milk to whole milk. Do not include this information in your report.

Be objective while reporting, not subjective. Objective means without emotion. Subjective means personal preferences, feelings, or emotions are clear in the report.

Use adjectives like bubbly, delightful, professional, rude, harsh, bright, loud, unhappy, slow, inefficient, or average.

Write complete sentences and do not start a sentence with "Yes, Bill said hello..." Just say "Bill said hello..." and leave the Yes or No out of the beginning of the sentence.

Use times and direct quotes to substantiate your shop. This creates a solid foundation and validates your findings.

If you state something is dirty, explain why it was dirty. Stating something is dirty does not substantiate your comment.

Be sensitive. If you must use terms to describe nationality, use terms that are considered politically correct.

Some companies have a specific way they like their reports written. Read the examples provided for each job for each company and write your report accordingly. Below are some examples.

(1) Space twice in between each sentence. Also, please make sure that you justify all "no" answers with a short comment.

(2) Space only once in between each sentence.

(3) Associate names cannot be written in your survey comments. Detailed information can be found in the shop instructions.

(4) Use past tense verbs.

(5) Write in first, second, or third person.

As you see, there are many types of report requests. Make sure to look at the sample provided by the company and read all the information.

Frequently Misspelled/Misused Words

A lot, No one: These are always two words.

Definitely, independent, knowledgeable, leisure, occasion, privilege, recommend, restaurant, vacuum: Spell these words correctly.

Nametag, name tag: Both terms are correct. Use the form that the company prefers by referring to your report form. If the company has used both variations, choose the one that you prefer. Be consistent: use only one spelling.

Probably: not prolly. I see this word used mostly on mystery shopping forums and, although the forums are casual places to talk with other shoppers, this makes the poster sound uneducated.

Ring, rang, and rung: Make sure to use the proper tense of this word.

Should *have*, could *have*, would *have* (not should of, could of, would of).

Then, than. Example: "We were seated in less than three minutes." Not "We were seated in less then three minutes."

Couldn't, shouldn't, didn't, wouldn't. These words should always be written out as "could not," "should not," "did not," and "would not."

Terms to Use for Narratives: Part One

Sometimes we get stuck in a rut when trying to describe positive and negative experiences. It is important to make sure we make each report sound fresh, new, and interesting to the reader. For example: "The associate was friendly during our interaction." Instead, you could write: "The associate was cheerful and enthusiastic during our interaction." Here are some positive terms to assist you while writing that exemplary report.

Positive words

Absolutely, Affable, Agreeable, Airy, Amiable, Appealing, Appetizing, Appreciated, Appreciative, Appropriate, Artistic, Attentive, Attractive, Bright, Bubbly, Carefully, Caring, Certain, Charming, Clean, Comfortable, Confident, Congenial, Conscientious, Considerate, Consistent, Courteous, Delicious, Delightful, Eager, Enchanting, Entertaining, Enthusiastic, Enticing, Exceeded, Exceptional, Exciting, Expertly, Exuberant, Eye-catching, Fascinating, Favorable, Flavorsome, Fresh, Genuine, Graceful, Honest, Immaculate, Immediate, Important, Informative, Interesting, Inviting, Jovial, Kind, Knowledgeable, Likeable, Lovely, Loyal, Manicured, Neighborly, Nicely, Orderly, Organized, Outstanding, Patient, Personable, Pleasant, Polite, Prepared, Professional, Prompt, Relaxed, Relaxing, Respectful, Satisfying, Sensational, Sincere, Skillful, Sparkling, Spotless,

Succulent, Superb, Tender, Thorough, Thoughtful, Tidy, Trustworthy, Unhurried, Welcoming, Well.

Terms to Use for Narratives: Part Two

Of course, not all of your reports are going to be positive. You will need ways to describe the not so good things that happen as well. This is actually harder than a good report. Good reports seem to flow while negative reports demand more thinking on your part as you have to sound non-emotional and offer only the facts. Your negative reports need to sound factual without being derogatory or inflammatory. Remember, the associates sometimes read your reports. If you must say something negative, do it constructively if possible. Read your narratives more than once when typing a report, especially a negative report, and make sure no signs of impartiality or emotion come through.

Here are some terms I hope you won't have to use too often. If you are not sure what words to use, look them up and make sure you have a full grasp of their meanings before using them. I cannot stress this enough. You do not want to use words you do not understand yourself.

Example:

Instead of writing: "The associate did not look at me; he made me feel rushed and kept looking at the screaming kid in the aisle."

You could write: "The associate did not make eye contact during our interaction. He was hurried and distracted by a screaming child."

Negative words

Abhorrent, Adverse, Agitated, Aloof, Ambiguous, Angry, Annoyed, Antagonistic, Bored, Careless, Casual, Cluttered, Confused, Contradictory, Contrary, Cramped, Crowded, Crude, Curt, Decayed, Defective, Deficient, Detached, Dirty, Disadvantageous, Disagreeable, Disappointed, Disarray, Discomfort, Discourteous, Dishonest, Disorderly, Disorganized, Disrespectful, Distant, Distasteful, Distracted, Doubtful, Dry, Dull, Dusty, Excessive, Forgetful, Foul, Gloomy, Greasy, Grimy, Harsh, Hasty, Hesitant, Hurried, Inaccurate, Inadequate, Inappropriate, Inattentive, Inconsistent, Inconvenient, Indifferent, Inessential, Inferior, Irregular, Irritable, Intrusive,

Invalid, Lacking, Lifeless, Messy, Monotone, Muddled, Mumble, Musty, Neglected, Nonchalant, Odor, Offensive, Overconfident, Preoccupied, Redundant, Refuse, Repelling, Reserved, Routine, Rude, Selfish, Scorn, Snide, Sordid, Speculative, Stubborn, Superfluous, Thoughtless, Tired, Tumultuous, Unappreciated, Uncaring, Uncertain, Uncommunicative, Uncooperative, Unconcerned, Unconfident, Undesirable, Uneasy, Unfavorable, Unfriendly, Unimportant, Unkempt, Unpleasant, Unsatisfactory, Upset, Vague, Vile, Vulgar, Withdrawn.

A last reminder: follow the narrative example given to you by the mystery shopping company you are completing the work for. This will give you a general idea of what is expected, but it should not be copied or used as a template as this may invalidate your report, causing it to be rejected by the company and you not getting paid. The only exception I have seen to this is with CoRI; they have one-sentence responses which they allow you to repeat in narratives you write for the same gas station client. Doing as I suggest will save you many headaches in the future.

Narrative Samples

Retail

The associate was looking directly at me and smiling as soon as I entered the store. She greeted me and offered assistance with a cheerful tone in her voice. She escorted me to the item I asked about, handed it to me, and offered additional assistance. She thanked me and wished me a good day before I left. As soon as I entered the store I was greeted by two associates. There was no mention of (xxxxx) at any time during my visit and no one was observed wearing a (xxxxx) button.

Additional registers were opened as soon as there were two or more customers in line. This saved me from waiting in line. Two registers were already open and more were opened as needed. There was no need to wait in line at any time during my visit. The cashier was friendly and cheerful. However, he did not ask about my (xxxxx) card, so I gave it to him after being offered my total.

This was a great visit. Both the associate on the floor and the cashier were personable and eager to assist me. The store was very clean and well organized, offering an excellent selection of items for the upcoming holidays as well as traditional hardware items. All items I checked were clearly priced. The cashier was great, but he did not ask for my (xxxxx) card. I would definitely return to this store and recommend it to others based on the great service it offered, the speed of checkout, and the selection of items.

Restaurant Sample #1

This sample shows how to write a non-naming report. Sometimes companies do not want you to use gender, names, or even their own product names in the reports. These are more difficult to write, so I thought I would share a report offered by one of my dear friends, Michele Shepard. This particular report allows for gender only. It is a great guide for many restaurant reports you may encounter.

Host/Hostess

When we arrived at the restaurant, the door was opened for us by an employee who was distracted. As we walked through the open door, the employee was looking the other way and did not say anything. She was not smiling and she did not make eye contact. We approached the host stand and another employee said: "Hello, two for dinner?" We told her that we had called ahead and she found our names on the list. She said it would take a few moments and she would call us when our table was ready. We told her we would wait at the bar. Less than ten minutes later, a third employee walked over toward us, called us by our names, and said that our table was ready. She told us to take care of our tab and come to her when we were ready to be seated.

We closed our tab at the bar and approached the waiting employee. While escorting us to our table she asked: "How are you tonight?" We replied and she followed up asking if we had enjoyed our holidays. We told her that we had and asked if she had enjoyed hers. She said: "I did, thank you for asking." By this time we were at the table and she pulled out a chair for the lady. She handed us the menus and pointed to the wine list. She told us our server would be right with us although she did not say who that would be. In parting, she said: "Enjoy your meal." She was smiling and friendly. She maintained eye contact at every opportunity.

Bar

When we approached the bar we saw two bartenders and five customers. We sat down and waited. One bartender was making drinks for the servers and the other had his back to us. Approximately one minute later he turned around and was surprised to see us. He placed napkins in front of us and asked what we wanted. He did not suggest anything. He did not say hello, or smile, or introduce himself. We asked for a bottle of beer and a rum and Coke. He said: "Double tall, it's happy hour." We were not sure what that meant and he did not explain. He turned to make the drinks and he served them fast. We watched him pour the rum into the glass without a jigger. He filled two-thirds of the glass with rum—it was a very strong drink. He did not say anything when he served the drinks. He simply put them down and walked away. He did not offer to start us a tab; nor did he ask our names.

He came back a moment later and asked if we wanted some bread. He followed up by asking if we were waiting for a table or going to eat at the bar. We told him we were waiting for a table. He did not offer an appetizer. Shortly thereafter, our table was ready and the bartender said he would transfer our tab to the server. We thanked him but said we would settle the bill with him. He asked if we were sure and we confirmed. He quickly placed the bill on the bar and we provided a credit card. Within seconds, he returned with the credit card slip to be signed. He placed it on the counter and said: "Thank you, enjoy your dinner." He then walked away. He did not invite us to return.

Server

Our server came to our table just over a minute after we were seated. He said "Hello" and said that he saw we had drinks from the bar. He asked if we wanted anything else to drink at that point. We requested a Sprite. He said: "Ok, I'll get that and some bread for you." He did not introduce himself; nor did he smile at any time during the meal. He never asked if we had been to <NAME> before; nor did he tell us anything about the restaurant. In one minute he returned with the Sprite, bread, and small plates. He poured the <RESTAURANT SPECIFIC> but did not say anything about it. He then asked: "Are you ready to order?" He did not suggest an appetizer so we ordered one. He then asked if we needed more time to decide on an entrée. We said we did and he told us he would put in our appetizer order and give us some time.

He never highlighted anything on the menu or made any recommendations. He returned in two minutes and asked if we were ready to order. We placed our orders and requested a straw for the Sprite. He had to go get a straw and return with it. He took our orders but did not repeat them back to us. He said "OK" and walked away. Our appetizer was delivered by someone else. The employee came to the table and said "<NAME>." We said yes, and he placed them on the table and walked away. He did not say anything; nor did he give us appetizer plates. When we were finished with the <NAME>, our server returned to collect the plate. Before he did he asked if we wanted to keep it to dip the bread into the remaining sauce. We declined and he collected the plate. Moments later, he returned with the salad and the soup. He put them down, said "Here you go," and walked away.

The next visit was from a different employee who served us our main course. The employee came to the table and said "Hi." He named the dishes as he handed them to us and he did know who had asked for what. He did not place both plates on the table. He held out the ladies plate until she took it from him directly; he placed the gentleman's plate on the table with the <NAME> logo upside down on the bottom. The salad and soup plates were not cleared so the table was cluttered. Approximately two minutes later, a waiter came over and asked if we needed anything. We asked for the extra sauce we had requested with our order. He said: "Oh, they didn't give you that" and quickly walked away. He returned with a bowl of sauce but no spoon to serve it. He said "Enjoy" and walked away. He took the salad and soup plates with him. The Sprite glass was empty for the majority of the meal and he never offered to refill it. He did not return to the table until ten minutes after we had finished eating. He asked if we wanted to box our leftovers and also if we wanted any dessert. He listed the desserts and we made a choice. In addition, we asked for another Sprite. One minute later he brought the Sprite and placed it down without a word. After seven minutes he returned with the dessert and two forks. He did not bring small plates for us to share the dessert.

When we had finished the dessert, he returned with the check. He asked if we needed anything else, placed the check carrier down, and cleared the dessert plate. He returned shortly to collect the credit card. When he delivered the receipt to be signed he placed it on the table and said: "Thank you very much, have a great night." We thanked him and he walked away. When we asked for the restroom he pointed across the dining room and said: "There's one door that leads to two doors." He never used our names. The food service and clearing was always carried out from one side of the table. We were not at a booth. We did not feel valued as customers and this waiter was not attentive during our meal. As we left, no one said anything and we opened the door ourselves to exit.

Manager

We observed two managers in the restaurant. They were both delivering food and bussing tables. One was wearing an apron and the other was not. They kept busy but we did not see either of them doing general table visits. Our table was never visited by a manager.

Food

The crab cakes were served on the edge of the plate with the sauce occupying the center. The sauce was perfectly spiced and the crab cakes were hot. They were garnished and the appearance was great. They were tasty and we would order them again. The soup was hot and spicy. It was served neatly in cups with no drips or spills. The taste was first-rate. The house salad was very cold and served on a chilled plate. The dressing was evenly distributed and the vegetables were crisp and fresh. The veal parmesan was attractively served. It was tender and had a very good taste. The spaghetti on the side was cold and had almost no sauce on it.

Some companies instruct you not to use names, genders, etc. in their reports, and the following is an example. Ruths Chris may have a steak called Ruths' Chris Sirloin. The company requests that their name not be used in the report. <RESTAURANT SPECIFIC> was fairly hot but the asparagus on the side was cold. There was very little cheese inside the chicken and half of it did not have any cheese at all. The sauce was smothering the chicken and it tasted wonderful. The brownie dessert was drizzled with chocolate sauce and attractively presented. It was cool in temperature and rich in taste. It was much more than two people could eat.

Cleanliness

The appearance and cleanliness of the restaurant, both interior and exterior, was excellent. We did not see any dirty areas. The landscaping was attractive and well maintained. We observed tables being cleaned immediately after the customers left. The restrooms were both clean and stocked. The lighting and temperature in the restaurant were comfortable but we did not hear any music.

Most people really enjoy the privilege of dining at fine restaurants like Ruth's Chris Steakhouse© and having their money reimbursed. Here is another example of what to expect when doing a fine-dining report. The report can be long, so give yourself ample time to do it. It is not uncommon to spend three or more hours on this type of report. This is courtesy of yet another dear friend, Servanne Edlund.

Restaurant Sample #2

The phone was promptly answered within one ring. Roselyn announced what location I had called and also introduced herself. She expressed herself in a positive, outgoing tone. I asked her until what time lunch was served and she confidently told me that it would be available until 4:00 pm. I then proceeded to ask her about any "specials" going on for lunch. She paused; I was not formally put on hold. In less than thirty seconds, after a little hesitation, she said that the specials were the small pizza and the crab cake sandwich. She was not rushed in her responses and took the time to answer all of my questions accurately. Upon ending the conversation, Roselyn told me that she would see me shortly for lunch and thanked me for calling. I felt very good about this call and thought it was handled in an excellent, professional manner.

Upon approaching the restaurant, I immediately noticed the bright colors used to paint the walls. It was eye-catching and inviting. The sidewalk was clean and all the doors and windows were free of smudges and fingerprints. I was also drawn to the many words written in French, such as "beer on tap" and "pig foot" among others. The French theme was well represented and no mistakes were found.

Ambiance

The restaurant had a lot of French influence from the Brasserie style of seating arrangement to the checkered table cloths. The background music was playing songs by such artistes as Jacques Brel, Edith Piaf, and Serge Gainsbourg. The music was loud enough to hear and understand the lyrics, yet soft enough to be able to carry on a conversation comfortably. The lighting was appropriate, enhancing focal points such as the quote from the movie *Silence of the Lambs* stating: "I like the French. They taste like chicken." The overall cleanliness of the restaurant was outstanding.

The restrooms were indicated with phrases painted on the doors. The restrooms were brightly lit and fresh smelling. There was a bouquet of flowers on the shelf above the sink. All necessary supplies were adequately filled. The fixtures were in proper working order. The powder room, overall, was clean and comfortable.

Host/Hostess

Immediately upon entering the restaurant, I was greeted by the hostess. She was not wearing a nametag. The first impression of the front door team was positive as both employees present behaved professionally. The hostess smiled and greeted me cheerfully. She asked me how many people were in my party and if a booster seat was needed. She immediately led me to the table, walking at a comfortable pace. When we arrived at the table, she waited until we were seated to hand us the menu. The menus were written on large sheets of heavy paper. They looked new and had no stains on them. Once she handed us the menus, the hostess wished us "Bon appétit" and walked away.

Server

Tina greeted us at our table within seconds of being seated at 1:50 pm. She did not ask if we had dined at this location before. She smiled and filled our glasses with water. She asked us what she should bring for the children as beverages and left right away. She came back with the kids' beverages at 1:53 pm and took the adults' beverage order. After returning with our beverages at 1:55 pm, Tina grabbed a stand on which the day's specials were written. She explained to us what the specials were and also announced the soup of the day. She informed us that she would give us a bit more time to look over the menu and left.

When she returned, Tina asked if we had any questions concerning the menu and I said I had. I inquired about the small cheese platter and she told me it was a personal favorite. Tina took our order at 2:01 pm. We received the appetizer as well as the items the children had ordered at 2:11 pm. A manager brought us the food, but did not place the correct entrée in front of the respective child. Tina checked back with us at 2:12 pm. She was prompt and pleasant and smiled a lot. The main course arrived at the table at 2:21 pm. The plates were passed on to Tina, who happened to be checking back on us. She placed the correct plates in front of the respective guests. The appetizer cheese platter was still on the table and was not taken away.

I ran out of iced tea early on but my glass was never refilled; nor was I offered another beverage. Once we were finished with the food, a gentleman who appeared to be a busser asked me if he could box the leftovers for me. It was 2:43 pm. I acquiesced and he returned with the box in a bag. Tina stopped by the table at 2:48 pm, asking if we would like a dessert menu. I ordered the dessert right away. It was brought to our table at 2:52 pm. As Tina asked if everything was fine, I asked for the check. She gave me the check at 2:54 pm. She was not ready to take my payment when I was ready to make it, and I had to wait for her. I had enough time to get my children dressed before she came back to take the payment at 3:00 pm. Although I paid with a credit card, my name was not used during the transaction.

Tina thanked me genuinely for my visit and wished me a great afternoon before I left at 3:01 pm. She maintained a positive, friendly attitude throughout our meal and was outgoing. She was pleasant to talk to. She appeared to be having a good time doing her job but seemed morose between interactions with her guests. Her overall salesmanship was good but she did not try to up-sell any items. I had a good experience and Tina made me feel valued as a customer during my visit.

Managers

The manager was seen all around the dining room helping the servers. One manager brought us the appetizer and the children's entrées. I observed another manager walking around the dining room, scanning the tables. The managers seemed to be enjoying their position and were present all around the dining room. They seemed helpful and exhibited a hands-on attitude.

Food

The Small Cheese Platter was served on a rectangular stone plate. It was a selection of three aged cheeses. I do not know what they were as Tina was not able to tell us. I guessed they were an aged Gruyere, a Gouda, and a goat cheese. They were served with a spoonful of honey, a few spiced walnuts and a little dish of candied figs. There were also three slices of toast smothered in aioli. The distinct garlic flavor of the bread created a perfect combination with the strong cheeses. The cheeses were of excellent quality and were accompanied with a few sliced apples and red seedless grapes. While the dish was not large, it was sufficient given the pungent taste of the cheeses.

The Bonjour Steak Sandwich was served on a slightly toasted Ciabatta bun. The thinly sliced steak was smothered with caramelized onions and Gruyere cheese. The dish was served at the right temperature and tasted delicious. It was accompanied with a large handful of fresh French fries. While the Ciabatta bread was a bit hard, the sandwich was of an excellent quality and the steak was juicy and tasty.

The Croque Monsieur was served on a ficelle baguette sliced in half. The bread was smothered with a rich and creamy béchamel sauce, topped with high-quality ham and smothered with Gruyere. It tasted scrumptious and was served hot and fresh. It was accompanied with French fries and I requested some Béarnaise sauce, which was delicious.

The Kids Cheeseburger and the Kids Mac and Cheese were served at the appropriate temperature. The cheeseburger consisted of a mini beef patty of excellent quality, cooked to a medium temperature and topped with a cheddar cheese. It was served with hot French fries. The Mac and Cheese was a rendition of the classic dish. It appeared homemade with high-quality cheddar and was served at the right temperature.

For dessert, I ordered the Crème Brule. It was served chilled and topped with three fresh raspberries and a leaf of fresh mint. The top of the Crème Brule was caramelized to perfection and was crusty.

The water we had was refreshing. It was pure and very clear. The iced tea was a delicious brew of dark tea, which made it refreshing and appeased my thirst. The selection of alcoholic and non-alcoholic beverages was extensive and offered a great value for the dollar. The selection of digestive drinks was impressive by its quality and diversity.

The baguette was more of a ficelle than a baguette. It tasted fresh, chewy on the inside and crusty on the outside. Accompanying the bread was a sweet butter cream with large grains of sea salt mixed in it.

This was my first visit to the Bonjour Bar Américain. It was a much better venue than most French-inspired restaurants. The overall quality of the meal and beverages was excellent. I had a very good experience with all of the staff members; they were all attentive and pleasant to deal with. The speed of service was excellent and definitely enhanced our experience. The restaurant was extremely child-friendly, with booster seats, highchairs, kids' menus, and crayons available. The authentic decor and ambiance added greatly to make it a memorable experience. For the nostalgia factor alone I would return! I wholeheartedly recommend this restaurant to those wanting to have a casual, Parisian Brasserie experience.

7 Company Notes to Shoppers

At TrendSource, we value the relationships we have with Field Agents who support our clients. We recognize the importance of the role that they play in our business processes and we do our best to listen to their feedback on how we can improve. We pride ourselves on being loyal to our Field Agents and always doing our best to make sure that there is enough work for them. Our expectations are simple—"Do what you say you will, and do it when you say you will." As a Field Agent for us, you need to understand your valuable role and purpose as a source of quality data for our clients. Clear, concise, objective and honest communication is required, along with a professional approach to assignments and this industry as a whole.

Jana De Anda, Senior Account Manager

Important Terms

Client: Credit bureau

Contact: Person to call and to meet during your visit

Executive suite: Many businesses located in a shared office space with one secretary

End user/authorized manager: Person you meet with

Marketing materials: Business cards, letterheads, flyers

TrendSource (MSI Services, Inc.)

MSI Services, Inc. is a sister company of TrendSource. All Independent Contractors are contracted to perform work directly with MSI Services, Inc. They are by far one of the easiest companies to work for. Their schedulers are quick to assist, their report forms are generally simple, and their requirement of narratives is minimal for most clients. This is the perfect company to work for if you are looking for clear and easy-to-follow questionnaires.

TrendSource refers to shoppers as "Field Agents." When you start their application process, it may seem as though they require more than other companies. Do not be intimidated and do not be afraid to give them the required documentation. Their site is secure and your information, including your social security number, photo ID, and bank information, is safe. You will not be required to give them this information until you have been accepted as a Field Agent.

They do not accept new shoppers until they have a need in your area; this is a huge benefit to shoppers as it prevents too much competition. Once you are an applicant, you will begin receiving e-mails with job offers. If you want to work for them, make sure to respond to these job offers quickly via e-mail. Once you have successfully completed a certain number of assignments, within their quality standards, you will receive additional privileges. So even if the job is not something you are particularly excited about, take it, learn, and get your initial jobs completed successfully so that you can take advantage of these additional privileges. You will not regret it.

TrendSource offers a large variety of jobs and I am always pleased to see new clients. Even when the economy is poor, the sales people at TrendSource work hard to get new clients. Some of their most common jobs are listed below.

Audits: There are a variety of auditing jobs available from Trend-Source. These can be revealed or covert, but generally they are more time-consuming than other jobs they offer, so be sure to set aside the appropriate amount of time.

Business verification jobs: These are simple jobs, but they are not your typical mystery shopping job. You will be meeting with a representative of the company, sometimes the CEO, and you must dress appropriately and represent TrendSource in a professional, business-like manner. You can gain additional privileges once you have proven yourself as a high-quality Field Agent. There are specific quality parameters that you must meet and you should refer to your TrendSource documents for these specifics. If you see one you would like to complete, apply for the job and contact their Support section if you have questions. You can also call their main number and ask for the extension of the scheduler in your area for business verifications. This is the time to ask questions if you are unsure of anything required. You must have a digital camera, not a camera phone, to complete these jobs.

Time is of the essence for these assignments; so as soon as you receive one of these jobs, make sure to complete the first steps as quickly as possible. Additionally, professionalism is of the utmost importance, so whenever you communicate with the contact via phone, make sure you are in a quiet location with no interruptions. Make sure to follow the script for the phone call that is provided on your Web site.

The contacts are generally aware you are going to be calling. In the rare event they are not, explain again why you are calling and respectfully answer their questions. Many times the contacts will not understand the purpose of the visit. Explaining the purpose will make the contact feel reassured and most will welcome the visit.

So what is the purpose of all this, you might wonder. In the compliance arena, public concern for data privacy has become increasingly visible through a surge of recent legislation. The consumer reporting industry has been largely impacted by such legislation, most notably through the Fair Credit Reporting Act (FCRA), which requires a third-party non-bias report of the state of a business's handling processes. I explain to them that the purpose of my visit is to make sure only businesses or persons such as themselves, which have a valid purpose and need, are allowed access to private information for consumers. Helping the customer understand the process and purpose of your visit will help assure that he/she has a positive experience, as well as welcoming you.

Tips for working at TrendSource

Be flexible and try to accommodate the contact's availability. If you are unable to meet their needs, work with them to set an appointment that will work for both of you.

Be prompt with all scheduled appointments. Account for traffic and if you are running late, call the contact and offer the courtesy of letting them know. They are running a business and time is valuable. Canceling or rescheduling a visit should be done only in an emergency situation.

Be prepared and make sure you have all the necessary paperwork and that your camera is in working order before leaving your house. Have a game plan in mind about what you will do first and how best to complete the inspection carefully and accurately. A good tip is to always take your photos in the same order (this will prevent you from missing a photo and having to return to the site).

Be professional and dress for success. You must wear business attire.

Be thorough and make sure you have reviewed each and every aspect of the Instruction Manual for this assignment. There are a number of specific items that are vital to the success of each assignment and you must be clear about the expectations.

Reporting your findings

As with all jobs, accuracy is of utmost importance. Checking off the wrong response can create a situation where either the business will not be approved by the contact or you will have to revisit for no additional compensation. It could lead to you not being assigned these types of jobs in the future.

Prepare your information prior to opening the report. Scan the required documents and resize all photos to meet MSI Services requirements. You can use a free photo-resizing program to do this. You can also rename the photo to organize yourself, if that helps.

Open the report, keeping only the report you are working on in front of you for accuracy.

Write in complete sentences.

Once you have entered your information, double-check it for accuracy. If anything out of the ordinary happened during your visit, make sure it is noted in the TrendSource comments to prevent questions at a later date. **Do not enter any information other than what needs to be expressed about the actual visit.**

Review the Instruction Manual to determine what needs to be uploaded for payment on these assignments.

Fast Food: TrendSource's fast food jobs often, though not always, include some type of reward for the employee. These jobs can be very satisfying for shoppers as you get the opportunity to potentially reward a job well done. Remember, you will have to reveal your identity, so choose these jobs carefully as you will not be able to return to this location for a while. If you give a cash reward to an employee, you will be reimbursed along with your regular pay. TrendSource has a reputation of being sensitive to shoppers who complete a number of these jobs and may accommodate the schedule for payments accordingly. However, *you should not take these jobs without knowing you can wait for the regular pay schedule*.

Grocery stores: These jobs are offered in several areas. They are simple, but some requirements must be followed. Make sure to read your manual carefully and take notes, or print it out for easy reference before entering the store. Never take your manual into the store! This applies to any store, for any company. Make sure it is hidden out of sight prior to leaving your car.

Tips for success

1. Fill out your note card in a similar fashion to the example below while you are looking at the job details on their Web site.
2. Remember that your job starts as soon as you get out of your car. Be prepared to be observant as soon as you step out of your driver's seat.
3. Remain in the store for the required amount of time. This will vary depending on the type of grocery store assignment you are completing. This must be done during the same time frame. You cannot leave the store and return to complete the required time. If you must leave for an emergency, when you return, calculate your required time from the beginning as if you had not been in the store earlier.

4. Make sure to take down notes in some type of code only you can recognize. This is to protect your anonymity in the event your notes are seen or lost during your shopping.

5. Keep detailed notes of the names and descriptions of all associates you encounter. There have been times when associates have worn the wrong nametag and if you have made note of their description, you can fall back on that to prevent you from not getting paid for the wrong associate name. Keep all your notes for six months.

6. Make sure you have visited all of the required departments prior to approaching the cash register. You can do this by mentally marking the end of your required time by visiting the restroom (if needed) after checking out all other departments.

7. If you have someone else with you on the visit, make sure they know prior to approaching the checkout lanes that this is **quiet time**. There is a lot going on during checkout and there is only one chance for you to get the information you need to accurately report the checkout experience. Put your receipt in a safe place immediately after it is given to you.

8. As soon as you enter your car, check your notes and make sure you have everything you need in order to report your findings accurately. Do not rely on your memory.

Phone jobs: These jobs are not normally posted. They are offered to field agents/shoppers depending upon location and past work history.

What if?

Q. I need to reschedule an assignment, the office is closed, and I cannot reschedule it from my Web site?

A. Utilize the Support process on your Web site. For the quickest response, make sure to utilize the drop-down options to properly align your message. You can type in exactly what you need to express to the scheduler.

TrendSource has a reputation of responding quickly to all messages. If it is the weekend and you need to reschedule, there is a chance no one will respond. **Always** complete the job the next day if you cannot reach someone, unless you have an emergency. In this case, you will have to wait.

I advise calling first thing Monday morning and speaking to the scheduler in addition to the message you have sent to Support.

Q. I forgot to get a receipt, now what?

A. Your receipt is proof that you have completed the assignment according to the program requirements. If you did not get a receipt, contact Support and they will provide instructions about how to proceed.

Q. How and where do I upload my receipt?

A. TrendSource's systems are very easy to use. Just follow the process required to enter your data and you'll have no problems uploading your receipts. Make sure to review the instructions available on your Web site about the requirements for size and clarity of your receipt, if you have any questions. You can use a digital camera or scanner to make a copy of it.

Q. When do they post jobs?

A. TrendSource posts jobs throughout the month and more than once a day.

Q. When do they pay?

A. TrendSource has a reputation of paying promptly. Their payment schedule is one of the advantages that they offer to their shoppers.

Q. Why do they require a photo ID?

A. This is required for legal and tax purposes, as well as for your own protection. They want to ensure that you are who you say you are.

Q. Who is my scheduler?

A. The best way to communicate with TrendSource is via their Support link. Use this tool to connect with the schedulers.

Q. What if I need to talk to someone?

A. Call the main number, press "0", and you will be connected to the operator. Be prepared with all the relevant information about your assignment so that the operator can connect you to the right person. If you have to leave a message for the scheduler, leave your name, Field Agent ID, phone number, assignment number, along with your question.

Sample note card

Store/location	Time in___	Time out___
Info	Info	Info
Info	Info	Info
Info	Info	Info

Corporate Research

Corporate Research International, Inc. was founded in 1997 in Findlay, Ohio, by its current President and CEO, Mike Mallett. Corporate Research International (CRI) began working exclusively in the multifamily housing industry in the late 1990s and was one of the first mystery shopping firms to integrate the Internet into their business model. Once released, CRI open up its product offerings to all industries including retail, restaurants, banks, convenience stores, and manufacturing. CRI was listed twice on the Inc. 500 fastest-growing private companies in 2005 and 2006. CRI is committed to excellence not only for its clients, but also for its shoppers.

Mike Mallett, President and CEO

Corporate Research is also referred to as **CoRI**. They offer a very large variety of jobs and most of their jobs and reports are simple. There are some exceptions to this, so do not self-assign a job until you have looked at the requirements and a sample of the report. Most of their jobs will start with very low pay. However, as the month goes by, the fees are raised on jobs that have not been taken. The tips listed below will help you to be successful in your working relationship with CoRI.

Tips for success working with CoRI

Stay positive. Do not assume that all the jobs they offer are low-paying. You can often do routes for CoRI and increase your pay significantly. I have done many jobs for them at more than double the pay seen on the job board. A route will generally consist of ten or more jobs of the same type. When you log into their system, if you see a large number of jobs all for the same client, click on the DETAILS for one.

You should see the scheduler's e-mail for that particular job. E-mail that scheduler and ask them whether or not they offer route pay for these jobs. Each client will be different so be prepared with job numbers when you do this, along with a date range. Once you have received a response and, if you find that routes are available, save that e-mail as suggested earlier in your company e-mail folder. This way, when you see new jobs posted, your contact information and the requirements for the routes are easily accessible. This will save a tremendous amount of time and prevent others from self-assigning the jobs while you are doing yet another search for the scheduler's contact information.

If you do not see an e-mail for the scheduler, call the number listed in Appendix C and politely ask the receptionist for the scheduler for that particular client in the state you're calling from. For example: "Hi, this is PamInCa and I would like to speak to the scheduler for xyz jobs in California." If the receptionist transfers you and you get a voicemail for the scheduler, simply press "0" on your phone and you will be reconnected to the receptionist. Ask if there is someone else you could speak with. Please remember the receptionist and the schedulers are literally dealing with thousands of shoppers throughout the day, so be courteous and ensure that you are remembered.

If routes are not offered and you really want to do a particular job, but the pay is too low, simply wait. Do not complain about how low-paying the company is, and do not give up on them as a potential employer. Only accept jobs that you deem reasonable for your time. Don't be intimidated by shoppers who post on mystery shopping forums stating you should only accept jobs that pay $10.00 or $20.00. And don't think you're the only one accepting those jobs. You only need to satisfy yourself. But I'm not suggesting doing one hundred jobs for $3.00 or $4.00, either!

My suggestion is to bundle jobs and make the most of your drive to a particular location. If you know you are going to be in a certain shopping center and you see a job that pays $5.00, which takes only a few minutes of your time to complete and report, add that job to your list if you can do it (on the same day you're working on the other job). Search the other self-assign companies and see if they have jobs in the area. It is much better to spend one hour at a shopping center or mall and make $50.00 with the pay and reimbursements option than to drive two hours and complete two $25.00 jobs requiring more extensive narratives. You will economize on gas, save the wear and tear of your car, spend less time on the computer, and make more money hourly by following this tip.

Try to schedule jobs and think in terms of hourly payment as opposed to what each job pays individually. If you remember, as mentioned at the beginning of the book, you have already figured out how much money you need to make. Try to stick to this but be flexible and realize that you, and only you, can make this happen. One day you may make more or less, but after a while you will see that it starts to balance out over the week.

CoRI is a great company to help you with this by adding some of their lower-paying jobs to your schedule, if you plan it right. CoRI posts many of their jobs a month or so in advance. This will help you plan shopping areas for the upcoming month. I have noticed over the last eight years of working with them that the jobs for the following month start getting posted around the 12th of the previous month. They add jobs throughout the month, but the 12th through the 16th is when the majority of their jobs are posted.

The narratives for their onsite visits are simple, requiring approximately 250 words. As always, type your narrative into a word document to check for spelling and grammar errors. Since there are a maximum number of characters allowed for their reports, you need to be able to delete and change wording easily. Sometimes, there simply isn't enough room to include everything you need to express about the visit. If you feel something must be included in the report, check the boxes under the questions to see if it can be included there. If not, check to see if there are any items in the report that can be deleted.

This company hires some great schedulers. Most of them will be more than willing to help you, work with you, and be there if you need them to answer questions. I cannot stress enough the importance of knowing who the scheduler is for every single job you do for this company. Keep track of the schedulers, their e-mails and phone numbers, as well as which jobs they schedule. Take this book with you when you are doing jobs so their phone numbers are easily accessible. If anything out of the norm happens while you're doing a job for them and it isn't covered in these tips, call. Do not try to make up your own rules and attempt to do the job in your own way. You will most likely not get paid.

Notice I said that the majority of the schedulers are great, not all of them. No company has a 100% success rate with schedulers. There have been a few occasions where the schedulers were not friendly with me or even somewhat rude. If you happen to come across a scheduler like this, don't be intimidated and don't argue. Neither will get you anywhere. Thank them for their time, hang up, and call back. Ask for one of the schedulers you have worked with in the past and ask their advice on the best way to handle the situation. This is rare but you need to be prepared. One bad scheduler can make a shopper stop working for a company and that's completely unnecessary. Even the supervisors have supervisors above them, so there is always someone to help the shopper.

With that said, if you do not do your job correctly, do not follow the instructions, do not take the right pictures, or fail to communicate, chances are that no one can help you. This is going to happen at some point in your shopping career. It happens to shoppers who have been doing it for twenty years, so don't get too mad at yourself. Dust yourself off and get back out there. You can ask to reshop the location at a later date. This will give you the opportunity to check other self-assign companies and add more jobs, so you are not in the hole too badly. Most importantly, take responsibility, be honest, and own your mistakes.

Don't wait for them to contact you; call or e-mail as soon as you realize your mistake and ask for help. Remember they are on EST (Eastern Standard Time) and they are available from 8:00 am to about 5:00 pm. There are schedulers who work in the second shift, which is generally from 3:00 pm to 11:00 pm. Find out who they are before you need them, and get their e-mails or extension numbers. There is also an online chat that is available Monday through Friday from 8:00 am to 10:00 pm, and on weekends from 11:00 am to 8:00 pm EST. CoRI has schedulers available to assist you by phone on the weekends from 11:00 am to 7:00 pm EST. Call the main line and after listening to the recorded message, press "1". This will connect you to one of the schedulers on duty.

CoRI completes thousands of jobs each month. Their editors are quick, but there are times when a job will still show as not being approved up to a week later. If this happens, it doesn't hurt to e-mail or call your scheduler after two days have passed to make sure the job has not been placed on error.

Let's cover some of their most common jobs and issues that occur. Some of these situations will arise with other companies as well and I would suggest following the same guidelines. Of course, you can always check with the actual company if they are open.

Gas station jobs: These jobs are great fillers. They require about ten minutes on-site and about ten minutes to fill out the reports online, once you know what you're doing. Don't be over-critical when evaluating the required areas for these jobs; this is a gas station, not a hospital. Remember to take photos to back up whatever you are noting down. Otherwise, you may not get paid. These jobs can be scheduled as a route. Generally the route will consist of twenty-five or more of these jobs within a certain time frame, at a higher fee than is shown on the job board. The scheduler will be able to tell you when the routes start for that particular month and how many you need to complete to get a certain fee. This requires nothing more than an e-mail on your part. ALWAYS include your auditor ID when e-mailing the scheduler, and a phone number for them to contact you, as well as your name. This will enable the scheduler to quickly read your e-mail and assist you in a timely manner. If you send your e-mails this way from the start, it will become a habit and will help you in the future with all your schedulers for the companies you contract with.

If you are doing a gas station job and the pumps are all closed for whatever reason, still complete the inside portion of the job. Prior to leaving, take at least two photos of all the pumps, showing they were not functioning. Sometimes they will have signs on them showing that they are out of order and these signs should never be handwritten, so this is something you would need to document in the report. Sometimes they will be marked off with cones or yellow caution tape. Again, this is something you need to note as all out-of-order pumps are to be properly marked with professional signage.

If you are unable to take a good photo of the pumps due to the associates being outside or watching out the front window, take the best photos you can or drive out of sight of the associate and take a photo from a distance. Explain in your report, under the appropriate section for the pumps, why you could not get a clearer or close-up photo. In addition, it would be wise to e-mail your scheduler for this job and let them know what happened. An example is given below:

"Hi Deb, I was completing job number 222777 today and all of the pumps were out of order. There were two associates working and one stayed outside the store throughout my visit. I took two photos from across the street as I could not get a close-up photo of any pump. I entered this information under the pump section in my report."

My auditor ID is 111111. PamInCa and my phone number is 777-777-7777.

Notice, I used the schedulers' name; I gave a brief description of what happened; the job number; my auditor ID; name and phone number. Most importantly, I told the scheduler where it was entered on my report, just in case the editor misses it.

If the restroom is closed or has an out-of-order sign on it, you still need to take a photo, preferably of the door showing the sign, which should not be handwritten. If it is you will need to enter this information on your report in the appropriate place. Ask the associate if they have a restroom, even if you see an out-of-order sign. You need to confirm this with the associate and enter the response in your report.

I have been in situations where the restroom was out of order and located inside the building where the associate could see me if I took a photo. If this happens, try to get behind one of the candy or snack counters and take a photo without using the flash. I have held my camera on the side of my leg, kept it inside of my purse and acted as if I was looking for my wallet, which of course I bring out after snapping a quick photo, holding it chest height, inside of my coat, to get a good view. I have also used my cell phone to take this kind of photo only and pretended to be talking. You will have to use your imagination. If you absolutely cannot get a photo without compromising your identity, take an overall exterior photo of the building prior to leaving the area and explain in your report the reason you could not get the required photo. The report will require one photo to be uploaded in the restroom section even if there is no restroom at the location.

If someone is using the restroom, even for fifteen or thirty minutes, you must wait. It is rare someone will be in there for more than five minutes, but if it does happen, you will need to wait without looking suspicious. You can pretend to be talking on your cell phone, looking at a map for directions, wash your windows, check your oil, or put air in your tires, anything that will offer you enough time to get into the restroom. Usually when someone has been in the restroom this long, it will not smell very good. This is not the fault of the station and should not be marked down. Be prepared, put a strong mint in your mouth, have your camera turned on before you enter the restroom, and take your photos quickly. But do not call for attention to yourself.

When marking down the restroom, pumps, or other areas, **be specific** as to what was wrong. For instance, do not just state that the restroom was dirty. Say instead that the sink was dirty/stained around the faucets. I use the terms dirty/stained together as sometimes it is difficult to determine which is more appropriate. If the toilet is dirty, state exactly where. For example: There was dried urine on the toilet in the front. With regard to the pumps, if the pump is dirty on the lower right side, state this; do not simply say the pump was dirty. This will reduce your chances of the editors coming back at a later time for clarifications or there are chances your job will not be accepted and you won't be paid. If you cannot get a single photo showing everything in the restroom, take one of the overall restroom, the best way you can. Then take one of the sink and one of the toilet and upload them in the additional photos section of the report.

If you arrive at a location and it is no longer in business, take two to four photos from various angles showing this. When you enter the report, you can upload any of the resized photos as your receipt. Remember, all photos should be the same size (640 × 480).

If you arrive at a location where there is no such address, take a photo of each address on the street, on the sides of where your station is supposed to be. For example: You are supposed to visit 123 Your Road. You find 124 Your Road and 125 Your Road, but there is no 123 Your Road. Take photos of both 124 and 125 Your Road. E-mail or call your scheduler and ask how to proceed. You will get paid for any closed location or incorrect address given to you, as long as you have proof.

If the associate is wearing a nametag, but it's covered by hair, a jacket or vest, state they were wearing visible nametags but the name could not be read due to whatever reason. In the section of the report which asks for a name, you can enter the words (jacket, hair, or vest covering nametag). Always explain your answers! If you cannot figure out where to put the information, e-mail or call your CoRI scheduler and ask for help.

Not all stations will be the same, but the report asks the same questions for all of the stations I have seen. I write my notes on the back of my receipt for each station. I put the name and description of the associate and answer whether or not they have the items or areas in the report, all on the back of my receipt. Abbreviations work wonderfully for this.

Some serve coffee or soda, and some have food counters. You must be accurate in your report. If the shop information states something is there that you did not find, make sure to state your findings in the correct location on the form. Some might not have a store, and others might not have self-serve pumps. If there is no store, complete all other parts of the job and state in your report that there was no store. If there are no self-serve pumps, do not get gas as you will not be reimbursed for it. Make your in-store purchase or restroom visit and as you are driving away, take at least one, and preferably two, overall photos of the station.

Pizza Jobs: Some of these jobs require photos and others do not. I cannot go into the details of which photos are to be taken due to my ICA (Independent Contractor's Agreement). So I am going to give you the best advice I can.

The jobs that do not require photos are very simple and will take you less than ten minutes to report. You do not need to leave your home as they are generally delivery jobs. If you see one of these that are in an area you are traveling to and you would like to complete it, you can ask the scheduler if you can have it delivered to another address.

Photo jobs are tedious and the photos must be taken **exactly** as shown in your training. If you take one of these jobs, be prepared to purchase what is needed in advance. It's called a breakaway knife. These can be purchased cheap, for around $2.00, at most local hardware stores. I have found the blades are good only for one job as they become dull very quickly; a dull blade will skew your efforts to cut the pizza the way it is required prior to taking your photos. Breakaway knives are serrated, so you can snap off dull blades to reveal a fresh blade for each job. Some shoppers have reportedly used box cutters with excellent results. Again, make sure the blades are very sharp.

I have found it easiest not to have hungry people around when doing this. It has taken me fifteen or twenty minutes to get the pizza cut correctly and take the **exact** photos required. Prior to preparing your pizza for photos, go to CoRI's Web site and pull up the job details. Click on the training link for these jobs. Follow it step by step. Do not omit any step. Print the steps if you choose, but I find it easiest to look at the photos offered in the training and move from one step to the next. There is a time frame for the photos to be taken so you will need to be efficient—another reason not to have hungry people around.

This job is one of the most difficult ones to complete properly for CoRI due to the photos element. The editors will cancel your job and you will not be paid if the photos are yellow, unclear, or not taken in the **exact** way they are shown in the training. Take several photos, upload them on your computer, and compare them with the ones in the training. Take additional photos if needed. Once you have mastered the art of taking the photos, do not become overconfident, and use caution each time. If you see your job has not been approved within a few days of reporting it, e-mail or call your scheduler to make sure the job has not been put on error. This may give you the opportunity to send additional photos if they are needed.

This job also requires a different type of receipt than other CoRI jobs do. Read your job details thoroughly and print everything you are required to print. I have seen this same job with other companies in the past; they have all required pretty much the same thing. So, if you like pizza, master this job, and you will be good to go if the jobs switch companies in the future.

Retail stores: CoRI offers a very interesting selection of retail stores, varying from hardware to upscale department stores. Each of them has their own specific requirements. Some are very easy with about eight questions, and others will require a visit to multiple departments and questions to be asked of associates. This will vary from one associate to eight, or maybe ten. You will need to read the details of the jobs before accepting any of them. Again, they may start out with low pay, but they too will increase the pay as the month goes by. The easy ones will be taken as soon as they are added to the job board and rarely increase their pay, so keep checking the job board.

Grocery stores: If you are lucky enough to live in an area in which you can visit their grocery stores, take as many as you can. These jobs are an exception to their normal low-paying status. They start off by paying fairly well from the very beginning. Although they require visits to multiple departments, they are easy and straightforward. The narratives required are generally minimal, comprising about 250 words.

Reporting

CoRI asks their shoppers to input the results the same day as the job is completed. If this is not going to be possible, contact your scheduler in advance, explain your situation, and ask for assistance. They can and almost always will extend your reporting date. If something unexpected happens on the weekend and you cannot get through to anyone and cannot enter your report, don't panic! E-mail both your scheduler and Support through their Web site to let them know what is going on. You will get late notices stating the job be removed from your list, but the system will generally not remove the job until 36 hours have passed. For this reason, I rarely take jobs for CoRI and schedule them on a Friday unless I am absolutely sure I will be able to complete them.

Why? If a job is scheduled on Friday and I cannot get the report to go through, I will probably not be able to reach anyone until Monday; 36 hours will have passed and the job will be removed automatically. However, great progress has been made in this area and they now have schedulers over the weekends and into the night. The key is to ask beforehand who you should contact if there is an issue over the weekend.

Finally, I believe this is one of the greatest companies out there. I highly recommend them and think they offer the largest variety of shops for new shoppers.

Market Force Information™

We at Market Force Information strive to provide a final product to our client that is second to none, and we understand that delivering a quality product begins with the work of our associates in the field. We are continually developing and innovating to offer our associates better ways to manage their assignments, communicate with us, and participate in new programs. Our contractors are serious about their work, and understand the importance of completing their assignments with integrity, and reporting the results in a timely manner. Market Force associates are able to choose from a wide variety of assignments, from mystery shopping to merchandising and theatre (movie) checking. We require dedication, commitment, professionalism, and a keen eye for detail.

Chris Owen, VP, Client Services & Systems Development
Market Force Information, Inc.
chowen@marketforce.com

Market Force Information offers an incredible variety of jobs and is the perfect company for new shoppers to get their feet wet. Assignments range from phone calls to theaters to learning about investments. This is a self-assign company, so you should check their job board daily because if assignments are not completed as scheduled by other shoppers, the assignments will reappear. They have jobs across the United States, in all US territories, and in Canada. They are extremely easy to work for and have a shopper support system that appears to be available almost every hour of every day. Once you have registered with them, make sure to look through their Web site carefully to become familiar with your options for assigning jobs, rescheduling, reporting, asking for help, and signing up for direct deposit. Shoppers who use direct deposit for payment will receive their money faster than those who receive payment by check. Market Force pays once a month for all jobs completed during the previous month.

Let's look at some ways to ensure your working relationship with Market Force is positive. Although they allow self-assigning of their jobs, they do not allow shoppers to continually assign and cancel jobs. They will remove you from their database if you abuse this feature. However, they will work with you if you have an emergency, so do not hesitate to reschedule a job if you need to. If you have to cancel a job, you can do so online, but I find it helpful to e-mail their help desk and let them know why as well. You can contact the help desk by clicking on the link below "Contact Market Force."

Only self-assign jobs you know you will be able to complete within the time frame and hours allotted. Most of their jobs have strict time frames in which they should be completed. In addition, Market Force only allows shoppers to complete a predetermined number of jobs for a particular client within a certain time frame, as well as a certain number of jobs daily for all clients combined. Read your paperwork carefully and if you are unsure, before completing a job for them, e-mail the help desk and ask.

Market Force requires accurate timings to the second for some of their jobs. These must be 100% accurate as the clients will sometimes review their video cameras to check the accuracy of the timings as well as the shoppers' comments. If your timings are incorrect, you risk not being paid, reimbursed or, worse, removed from Market Force's shoppers' database. You must use an accurate timing device. Practice working with the timing device several times before attempting to use it on a job.

Since they have such a large variety of jobs, their reports are just as varied. Some require no narratives, whereas others need to be extensive, such as bank reports. I do not recommend starting out with bank jobs for this company or any company until you have become more familiar with what is required for narratives on these types of reports. It can be overwhelming and frustrating for new shoppers. Make sure to read the job description and requirements carefully before self-assigning a job. I cannot stress this enough.

Reports for Market Force are due no later than twelve hours after the assignment has been completed. If you have computer issues or anything else that may affect your reporting within this time frame, you **must** contact them either by using the help desk e-mail or by phone. In addition to the report, you will need to scan or take a picture of both the receipt and the Contractor Payment Invoice (CPI). You will need to upload these after you have completed your report in order to get paid. You can do this directly after entering your report or from the link on your home page. This must be done within the same 12 hours as is assigned for submitting the report. You can check to see if both the receipt and the CPI have been accepted by clicking on the CPI/Receipt Status Page. If one or both are not accepted, you can resubmit them using the Scan CPI/Receipt link. Not all reports will require both; again, carefully read the requirements for each job.

Currently, there are two login portals on the Market Force Web site and you must be registered through both portals to access all assignments. The assignment tasks vary by assignment type, but the general guidelines, including communication, canceling, and reporting your results within 12 hours, apply to all assignment types.

Service Intelligence/Experience Exchange

Service Intelligence is a North America-wide company that focuses on partnering with clients to give them the best in clear and actionable data, to help them achieve their corporate goals. Working with some of the top mystery shoppers in North America, we continue to strive to improve and expand our services to our clients and provide a wide variety of mystery shopping opportunities for our contractors: from restaurants and convenience stores to educational institutions and major retailers, and everything in between.

As one of the top mystery shopping companies in North America, we take pride in attracting and training the best mystery shoppers.

Mark Hilborn, VP and General Manager
Service Intelligence

Service Intelligence (SI) offers a large variety of jobs. Some are self-assign and others are listed as subscriptions. They pay once a month and are leaders in the business of mystery shopping. This is one of the first companies you should apply to.

Certifications

All the jobs you take will require you to get certified for each particular client. The certification page can be found by clicking on the link at the top of your login page. Once you open this page, it will list the clients and show whether or not you are certified. Click on the appropriate client link and you will find all the instructions for that particular job. Take all the certification tests for the clients you are interested in that have locations near you. You do not need to take all certification tests as some clients may not be in your area. You may still have to take a refresher test before being able to select the job, but it will be much shorter.

If you have taken the tests too many times without passing, you will need to contact your program delivery specialists (PDS) and ask for assistance. This only applies to certain programs, but you need to be prepared. Remember, click on the appropriate client when contacting your PDS.

Opening the certification page for Service Intelligence/Experience Exchange

Make sure the pop-up blocker is turned off. It will appear at the top of your computer screen. Generally it has a different color and easy to see. If this doesn't work, contact field support at the top left of your home page on The Experience Exchange website.

Project Review

Before you accept a job or take the certification quiz, you can check the specific job requirements by looking at the project review. Open the same page as for the certifications and click on the client you are interested in. At the top of the page, click on tips. This will give you an idea of what the job entails. You can also get an overview by clicking on View next to the actual job you are looking at in available assignments.

Once you have accepted an assignment, if you want to review the project tips, click on Jobs To Do at the top of the home page. This will show your job. Click on the correct one, scroll down, and you will see a bar at the very bottom of your job. Move that all the way to the right and you will see your options if you scroll back up to the job. It will appear right before the word Go. You'll see a drop-down menu.

PDS

The schedulers at SI are called program delivery specialists (PDS). If you have a question for your PDS regarding one of your jobs, you can contact the correct one by using the Contact field support button on the top left of the login page. Click on New Message, this will offer a drop-down menu by client. You can type in your question in the large box below. Be prepared with a job number and subject. Opening this page will not close your Job to Do page, so you can go back and forth to make sure you have the right job number, etc. When the PDS responds to your question, you will generally get an e-mail letting you know you have new messages from SI. Log in and you will see New Message in the center of the page. Click on that and it will take you to your question; below that will be the answer from the PDS.

Selecting Jobs

SI limits shoppers to ten jobs a month when they are new. This is a rolling limit. Here is how it works: You select ten jobs, you complete five, you can then select five more. After you have completed jobs for them, if you want to take on more, send a message through the field support for the particular client you want to do the job for. They will increase the number of jobs you can do for them gradually, if you ask. This is not automatic, you must ask.

You can do as many jobs as you choose for the same client in one day; as long as you stay within the time frames, job completion can be as long as you stay the required amount of time for each one. Most jobs will require a minimum of twenty minutes at each location. Remember, each client requirement is different; make sure to read your guidelines carefully.

Once you have completed the certification for the jobs you want, you can self-assign any jobs on the board for that client. You will generally be limited to six of the same type of jobs in one month. You can ask for more through the support link. You do not need to complete all the certifications, only the ones for the jobs you are interested in.

When there are more than 100 jobs available in the state, you can select all the cities listed with the number of jobs in each city. Check off the cities you want to search and the jobs will appear. You can self-assign any of the jobs listed.

Subscriptions

SI offers a subscription program. Simply put, this is a pre-assign option. You are not automatically guaranteed a job by subscribing to it. Click on the subscription tab at the top of the page. This will open a new window. Your address will appear, along with a number in the search radius. Change this number to fifty or higher to offer you a further radius search. This will list all the jobs in your selected radius search.

If you are interested in doing a job on a regular basis, subscribe to it and to as many others as you would like. You will get an e-mail when the job is offered to you. You can then accept or decline this offer. If you decline a job offer three times, you will be removed from that subscription. This is separate from the self-assign jobs; from what I have seen it doesn't affect the jobs you can self-assign.

If you have taken your certification tests and still cannot self-assign a job, make sure you have entered your Automatic Bank Deposit (ABD) information on the Web site. Until you enter this information, you will be unable to select any jobs. You must have a bank account and provide your bank account information. They are completely secure and can be trusted with this information.

To see your invoice, click on the My Invoice at the top of the page. You might see two invoices depending on how long you have been working for them: the previous month at the top and the current month at the bottom. Service Intelligence pays monthly by direct deposit only.

The majority of their jobs require a receipt or business card to be submitted. They may soon require all jobs to include a receipt or business card, per their director. You must keep all receipts for this company for a minimum of six months. There is generally an e-mail address in your job instructions giving you this information. Read your instructions carefully and if you have a question, send a message through Support.

If you receive an e-mail from the PDS regarding available assignments, you do not need to respond if the jobs are not in your area. However, if they ask you through the Message Center, good manners require a polite acceptance or decline of the offer.

Entering Your Completed Job

Once you have completed a job, log in and click on Jobs to Do. All of your jobs will appear. Click on the job you have completed and scroll down. Again, you may have to move the bar on the bottom all the way to the right to see where the Enter Job tab is. Click on it and your report will appear. Enter your information, check it for accuracy, and hit Check and Submit. If there are errors, a box on the left will appear telling you what needs to be fixed. Although a few reports may show an error, it really isn't an error, just a glitch in the Web site. Hit Ignore This Warning and it will go through. I cannot go into more specific details regarding this due to my Independent Contractor's Agreement (ICA). Make sure you have entered the correct information prior to hitting Ignore This Warning.

Media Upload

This is the simple process of uploading photos to SI's Web site for jobs requiring pictures to substantiate your findings. Make sure your photos coincide with your answers on your evaluation form. There is a special test for media upload. It is at the top of the certification tabs. If you have never submitted photos through media upload, you will need to be activated to do so. Send a message through the support center with the Media Upload link and ask to be activated. You need to wait to be notified that you have been activated. If you need help with it, contact the PDS through the field support link. If you still have questions or problems, call them.

If you arrive at a location that is closed, you still need to fill out the evaluation form and submit the job as closed. SI pays a reduced fee for a closed job; since there is no purchase made, no reimbursement will be made.

Remember, just like all other companies, mileage, office supplies, etc. are not reimbursed. Figure in this cost when accepting all jobs.

8 New Shopper Support

You may find yourself in predicaments from time to time, so make sure to carry this book with you so you have your company emergency contact numbers. Always call the company if you are unsure of anything. They are always willing to help shoppers be at their best and do their jobs correctly for their clients.

I thank you for buying this book and wish you all the success. If you have a question that has not been covered here, feel free to e-mail me. I have set up an e-mail account just for you: **paminca@ymail.com**

Terms

Active sampling: The simple act of an employee offering a food sampling.

Amenities: Features of apartment, offices, hotels, and casinos offered to guests or residents. Examples:

Tennis courts, swimming pools, business centers, exercise facilities, Jacuzzis, parking facilities.

Anyone shop: Means you can shop anyone you encounter. There is no specific person required to be shopped. This is the opposite of a targeted shop.

Associate: Employee. These words are interchangeable. However, if the company uses one term or another on the questionnaire, use the same one. Example:

Question: Were all associates wearing nametags?

Shopper narrative response: All associates were clearly wearing nametags. Do not say all employees were clearly wearing nametags. Keep your wording the same throughout the reporting process.

Audit: Inspection of a building or facility, or the products within the building or facility.

Audit shop: Announced visit where you will be given specifics to examine and report back on.

Benefit: A product or service benefiting the consumer. A benefit is why the product or service is beneficial to you. Examples:

Purchase the telephone and you will get a free GPS system.

If you join now, you will get 6 months of free service.

Bollard: Heavy posts or guard rails that protect something. Generally these are used to keep cars from hitting something. This term is commonly seen in gas station reports.

Branded: The company or site you are visiting will have a physical display of the company name or logo on the building or the associate's uniforms. Example:

Burger Queen might have cups with the Burger Queen logo as well as the associates wearing uniforms or hats/visors with the Burger Queen logo on it.

Business hours: The time during which the business is open to customers.

Business casual: Exhibiting an overall, clean, neat appearance. No sandals, shorts, flip-flops, revealing clothing, visible tattoos, or piercings other than in the ears.

Buyback: The end of semester when the students sell textbooks back to the store.

C-Store: Abbreviation used for a convenience store.

Candy striping: Means that the products are intermixed.

Canned response: A prepared response. This can be used by an associate, for example: "Hi, welcome to Burger Queen." This is said to each and every customer and there is no change made by the associate at anytime. Or it can be seen on a mystery shopping report in your questionnaire, which means there are a variety of predetermined answers for you to choose from which best reflect your experience.

Cart corral or corral: The area in which all store carts are stored or placed in the parking lot or at the front of the store.

Chronological order: Details of an event or visit given in the order they happened.

Claim check: Ticket or receipt given for later pick-up. Examples:

Valet parking, coat check, or dry cleaners.

Cookies: A small file or part of a file stored on a web user's computer, created and subsequently read by a Web site server, containing personal information such as a user identification code, customized preferences, or a record of pages visited.

Clarification: To make certain information reported is accurate. Example:

Are you sure all associates were wearing nametags?

These clarifications will generally come from an editor and require an immediate response.

Clarifying question: Simple question of fact. Example:

Does this only come in red?

Close-ended question: Question that can be answered with yes or no. It requires no further dialogue between you and whoever you are speaking with.

Community: Generally the area in and around apartment or office complexes.

Competitors/Competitor shops: Companies that provide the same or similar products.

CPI: Contractor payment invoice.

Cross merchandising: When different items of a related field are positioned together in a display, such as printers, ink, and paper.

Dedicated planogram: Also known as **"blocked"**: A section of merchandising display space where items of only one product are grouped together. A dedicated planogram could be any particular display, store branded display, etc.

DVR: Digital voice recorder. Found at office supply shops.

Exterior: The area outside of a location, up to the entryway.

General needs question: Broad, general question asked by an employee to determine your needs.

Gender-specific: Male or female. Generally, companies request you not to use terms revealing the sex of the associate.

Feature: Answers a "what" question. Example:

This television is HD ready.

This camera has automatic focus.

Framing: Means that a competitor's product is positioned on top, at the bottom, and/or on the sides of the corresponding name brand product.

ICA: Independent Contractor Agreement. Should be read thoroughly and taken very seriously. Companies use this to protect themselves and they can and probably will remove you from their database of shoppers if you break this agreement. Each company will have its own version; do not assume you know what it says. You must sign one for each company you work for.

Indirect close: When an employee tries to sell a product in a situation where the agent asks for an opinion without asking for a firm commitment. Examples:

Do you think your furniture would fit in this room?

Should I take this to the front for you?

Island or Fueling island: The area where fuel pumps are located on the exterior lot of a gas station. Generally, a fuel island will consist of several pumps grouped together on a raised concrete pad.

Itemized receipt: A receipt that lists each item purchased and its cost. Not a credit card slip.

Horizontal merchandising: Merchandising where a non-name brand product is displayed either above or below the name brand product.

ID sign: Sign displaying a store's logo.

Indirect close or Trial close: When a leasing consultant, car salesman, or store associate attempts to "close the deal" indirectly. This can be done by stating that vacant units rent quickly or that another person is also interested in the unit. Examples:

Should I take this to the front for you?

Should I get the paperwork started?

Kiosk: A small structure that takes the place of a full-scale store.

Landscaped areas: The exterior area of any location, including all lawn areas and plantings.

Leasing consultant: An employee of an apartment community, furniture rental, car rental, etc.

Live: Cartridges or other products are displayed on the sales floor and customers can serve themselves.

MFO: Motor fuel only. Refers to a gas station that sells gas only; no other items are offered.

Model: An unoccupied structure, home, apartment, etc., usually furnished and decorated, that employees use to demonstrate features to prospective tenants or buyers.

Non-Branded: When a company does not have their name or logo displayed **anywhere** at the location.

Objective: 1. Something that one's efforts or actions are intended to attain or accomplish.

Objective: 2. Expressing and reporting facts or conditions without distortion by offering personal feelings, prejudices, or interpretations.

Open-Ended Question: A question that cannot be answered with yes or no.

Phishing: In the field of computer security, phishing is the criminally fraudulent process of attempting to acquire sensitive information. This could include usernames, passwords, and credit card details, by masquerading as a trustworthy entity in an electronic communication.

Planogram: A display space holding products arranged in a specific manner or order.

Product knowledge: Confident understanding of a subject or piece of merchandise.

POP: Point of purchase. Cash register.

QC reviewers: Quality control reviewers. Editors.

Rapport: Creating a friendly relationship marked by ready communication and mutual understanding.

Reimbursement: A set amount of money given back to the shopper to cover the cost of the required purchase.

Resolution: A measure of the sharpness of an image or of the fineness with which a device (e.g., a video display, printer, or scanner) can produce or record such an image.

Reman: Remanufactured ink cartridges and toner cartridges are previously used cartridges that have been reconditioned. Most store-branded cartridges (e.g., OfficeMax, Office Depot, Staples) are remanufactured.

Rush: The beginning of the semester when all the students are purchasing books for their classes at the same time.

Selection guide: A preprinted product guide that defines products and their corresponding use.

Signage: Signs present at the location.

SKU: Specifically the number a product is designated within a store to differentiate it from other products. Each differentiable product has its own SKU. This is the bar code you see cashiers scanning.

Specialty media: Photo paper.

Spoofing: Fraudulent e-mail activity in which the sender address and other parts of the e-mail header are altered to appear as though the e-mail originated from a different source.

Take-a-ticket: Merchandising method where a ticket for the product, not the product itself, is displayed. This ticket is taken to a sales associate who gets the respective item for the customer.

Target shop: A shop in which you must interact with a specific person.

Upload: The act of transferring a file from your computer to a company Web site.

Up-Sell or Suggestive sell: When an upgraded or more expensive item/service or an additional item/service is suggested to a customer.

Video shop: A mystery shopping job that requires the use of a hidden video camera.

Wing cap: The same as an "End Cap.": a display located on the end of an aisle perpendicular to the aisle's products.

Resources

The information in this chapter has been gathered from years of dealing with a variety of issues and the best ways I have found to best work with and around them. A list of tips to make reporting the jobs you complete easier is also provided.

Computer:

Windows XP© help: http://tinyurl.com/5emv8 (http://www.microsoft.com/windowsxp/using/ setup/getstarted/bott_fstw.mspx)

Microsoft©:
http://www.microsoft.com/en/us/default.aspx

Adobe©: Some forms will require Adobe© reader. This program is free and you can download it from this site: http://get.adobe.com/reader/

Efax®: http://www.efax.com/about-us

PDF file saver: This will allow you to save your completed reports online. It is free, but must be downloaded: http://tinyurl.com/2scjk (http://www. cutepdf.com/Products/CutePDF/writer.asp)

Excel: Some forms will be sent to you in an excel program. You may also want to have a spreadsheet for your jobs. These sites will help you:

http://www.usd.edu/trio/tut/excel/
http://excel.tips.net/

Excel viewer:

http://tinyurl.com/7ylmb (http://www.microsoft.com/downloads/details.aspx?familyid = c8378bf4-996c-4569-b547-75edbd03aaf0&displaylang = en)

Resizing pictures:

Microsoft© offers a free program to resize photos that will avoid opening each photo and resizing it. This only works for Windows XP©: http://tinyurl.com/2meyw (http://www.microsoft.com/windowsxp/downloads/powertoys/xppowertoys.mspx)

If you don't have Windows XP©, download from: http://bluefive.pair.com/pixresizer.htm

For McIntosh©: http://www.gimp.org/macintosh/

If you don't have Microsoft Office©, you can use this site to download many of the same types of programs: http://www.openoffice.org/ http://why.openoffice.org/why_sme.html

Free antivirus programs

Avira—There is a free program and a paid program. The free program is great, but you will get a pop-up each day asking if you want to buy the paid program: http://www.avira.com/en/pages/index.php

AVG—There is a free program and a paid program: http://www.avg.com/

Free Wi Fi sites for traveling and reporting:
http://www.wififreespot.com/
http://wi-fi.jiwire.com/

Printer:

Before buying a printer, check the costs of ink refills. You will need to replace them often. Laser printers will print more and last longer than ink-jet printers. You can order ink from PrintPal© for most printers, and it is much cheaper than in the stores: http://www.printpal.com/

Save on printer ink by using draft or quick print, which you will find in your printer information. Print two or more pages on one sheet of paper by printing on one side, turning it over, and using the other side. You may be able to set your printer up to automatically print on both sides of the paper. To check this, click on **My Computer**, **Control Panel**, and **Printer**. Your computer may be a little different and you can click on control panel without going into my computer first. Open the printer by clicking on the icon. Click on preferences, click on fast draft, black ink only, and if needed two-sided printing.

Changing your e-mail:
http://www.freshaddress.com/stayintouch.cfm

Calendars:
http://www.printfree.com/Calendars.htm

For finding out all the **zip codes** in the areas you like to visit, these sites are the easiest to use: http://www.zip-codes.com/
http://zip4.usps.com/zip4/citytown.jsp

Online dictionary and thesaurus:
http://www.merriam-webster.com/netdict.htm

Roboform©: This software must be downloaded. It will save passwords and forms, and do many other time-saving tasks for you:
http://www.roboform.com/

If you have a **GPS** system, use it. It will save you an incredible amount of time. You can enter all your jobs for the day into it in the morning and move from one location to the next with ease. If you do not have a GPS, you can try Microsoft's© Streets and Trips for free for 60 days:
http://www.microsoft.com/Streets/en-us/default.aspx

DVR: Digital voice recorders can help you remember timings, names, and other valuable information while remaining anonymous.

Taxes: You are responsible for your own taxes. Many of your questions can be answered from the IRS Web site:
http://www.irs.gov/businesses/small/index.html

Company Web site issues:

If you click on a Web site and get a "This page cannot be displayed" message, don't panic; try it again. If it still doesn't work, go to Internet options in your tools at the top of your computer screen. Delete cookies and temporary files, and clear your history. I do this weekly to keep my system a little cleaner. Try the Web site again to see if others are having the same issue. If no one has posted an issue there, do a search from the top right of the page by entering the company name only, and post the issue you are having under the correct company header. If no one has posted any issue about this company before, start a new thread. Make sure you have searched carefully first.

E-mail the scheduler to make sure they are aware of the problem. Copy and paste what error message you are getting into the body of the e-mail so they can send it to their IT department if necessary. Once the company is open, call them using the phone numbers listed in the back of the book. Remember, communication is the key.

Taking photos: Always take your photos in the same order for every job you complete; this will make finding them and connecting them with the correct job easier.

Letter of authorization: It is a good idea to print a copy of your assignment if you are not offered a letter of authorization by the mystery shopping company. This will save you many headaches if you are caught taking discreet photos or measurements, or anything required of you that might make you look suspicious to employees or even the police. I have been asked several times by police officers what I was doing when I was caught taking photos. Do not get nervous; simply explain who you are and why you are there. Present them with the letter of authorization or copy of your assignment sheet.

Get up early: There are a lot of companies on the East Coast that have jobs across the United States. If you live in a different time zone, get up early to get those jobs.

Be the **BEST** shopper: Stand out from the rest by proving your dependability each and every time you work for a company.

Make your job easier: If you are completing a report that has several boxes in which to mark yes or no, check all of the yes answers prior to completing the job. This way, when you go back to complete the report, you can change only the no responses as needed.

Mystery Shopping Company List[3]

The companies listed below with an **(S)** next to them allow self-assigning of jobs. For some of the companies, you may have to complete a certain number of jobs before being allowed to self-assign. Some may change their programs, so make sure to adjust this page as changes take place. The companies listed with an **(E)** next to them are those that require relatively simple reports without too many narratives. Remember, your first contact should be via e-mail, rather than calling a company. Use these phone numbers only for emergencies.

A & A Merchandising Ltd.©:
http://www.aamerch.com/, 416.503.3343

AboutFace©:
http://www.aboutfacecorp.com/newindex.html,
877.770.8585, 678.989.2290

A Closer Look© (S):
http://www.a-closer-look.com/, 888-446-5665

---

3. **Disclaimer:** This is a list of companies that offer mystery shopping. It is NOT a list of recommended companies as I have not worked for all of them. Search on Volition.com for feedback on these companies before you do any work for them.

A Customer's Point Of View©:
http://www.acpview.com/, 770-288-2717

Advanced Phone Ups©: http://phoneups.com, 800-285-0026, 805-383-9912

Advanis—No © or ® on Web site: http://mysteryshopper.advanis.ca/, 888-944-9212, 780.944.9212

Affinity Services©: http://www.affinitymarketingservices.com/, (616) 243-6095

A Step Above Service Evaluations©, http://www.serviceevaluations.com/—No phone number available

ABA Quality Monitoring Ltd.—No © or ® on Web site: http://www.aba.co.uk/ + 44(0)161 431 1234

Absolute AdvanEDGE, LLC—No © or ® on Web site:
http://www.absoluteadvantedge.com, 303-814-2382

ACE Mystery Shopping, LLC©: http://www.acemysteryshopping.com/ 866.240.7324 Toll Free | 866.662.5642 Toll Free Canada

Acorn—No © or ® on Web site: UK:
http://www.acorn-ma.co.uk/index_main.html, + 44(0)151 355 2657

Affinity Services, LLC©: http://affinityservicesllc.com/index.html, 303-955-5627

AIM Field Service—No © or ® on Web site: http://www.patsaim.com/, 407-886-5365

Alexandria's Marketing—No © or ® on Web site:
http://www.alexandriasmarketing.com/, 574-243-1907

All-Star Customer Service, Inc.©: http://www.allstarcustomerservice.com/ 817.295.3013

Aloha Solutions, LLC©: http://www.alohasolutions.net/, 704-821-6180

Amusement Advantage© ®: http://www.amusementadvantage.com/, 800-362-9946 option 5

Ann Michaels & Associates Ltd.©: http://www.ishopforyou.com/, 630-922-7804

Anonymous Insights Inc.—No © or ® on Web site: http://www.a-insights.com/, 614-761-0939

Anonymous Shoppers & Assessments (ASAP)—No © or ® on Web site: http://www.asapittsburgh.com/index2.htm, 412.831.1227, 972-406-11,04

Apartment Shoppe—No © or ® on Web site: http://www.apartmentmysteryshopper.com/, 816 523 3793

Apartment Shoppers Plus, LLC©: http://www.apartmentshoppersplus.com/, 763-550-0606

AQ Services International©: http://www.aq-services.com/, United Kingdom: + 44 (0) 20 7908 6702, Europe: + 31(0)70 331 95 00

Ardent Services—No © or ® on Web site: http://www.ardentservices.com/, 303-525-8892

A Top Shop©: http://www.atopshop.com/, 720-283-8377

Automotive Insight, Inc.—No © or ® on Web site: http://automotiveinsightinc.com/home.html, 239-949-5950

At Random Communications (ARC)—No © or ® on Web site: http://www.arllc.com/index.asp, 800-993-6093, 860-672-0606

At Your Service Marketing©: http://www.aysm.com/, 800-410-5396, 940-644-2893

ATH Power Consulting© ™: http://athpower.com/, 877-977-6937

B. Business Solutions Inc.—No © or ® on Web site: http://www.bizshoptalk.com/, 570-474-2212

Baird Consulting Inc.©: https://baird-consulting.clientsmart.com/, 920-563-4684

Bare Associates International©: http://www.baiservices.com/, 800-296-6699

Barry Leads & Associates/Informa Research Inc.©: http://www.barryleedsassoc.com/, 800-848-0218

Benchmark Collaborative—No © or ® on Web site: http://www.benchmarkco.com/, 888-249-9606

Berring Hine—No © or ® on Web site: http://www.berring.co.uk/html/mkt_research.html, 020-7432-0350

BestMark Inc.© (S, E): http://www.bestmark.com/, 800-969-8477

Beyond Hello Inc.®: https://www.beyondhello.com/secure/index.htm, 800.321.2588/608.232.1414

Beyond Marketing Group Inc.©: http://beyondmarketinggroup.com/, 336-722-6270

Bevinco—No © or ® on Web site: http://www.bevinco.com/, 888-BEVINCO, 416-490-6266

Big K Mystery shopping—No © or ® on Web site: http://www.bigk.com.mx/—No phone number available/ Spanish, info@bigk.com.mx

BMA Mystery Shopping—No © or ® on Web site(S): http://www.mystery-shopping.com/—No phone number available

Brand Marketing International, Ltd. (BMI): http://www.brandmarketingltd.com/, 941- 379-5611

Business Evaluation Services©: http://www.mysteryshopperservices.com/, 888- 300-8292

Business Insights Group—No © or ® on Web site: http://www.businessinsights.com/, 754- 775-7227

Business Research Group—No © or ® on Web site: http://www.businessresearchgroup.net/, 248-642-6400

Business Research Group UK—No © or ® on Web site: http://www.brg.co.uk/, United Kingdom- + 44 20 8832 7750, China- + 86 10 6562 9095

California Marketing Specialists—No © or ® on Web site: http://www.sassieshop.com/2californiamarketing—No phone number available

Campaigners, Inc.©: http://www.campaigners.com/, 310-643-7500

Campus Consulting©: http://www.shopaudits.com/, 604- 736-1869

Capstone Research©: http://www.capstoneresearch.com/, 973-575-6161

Certified Marketing Services (CMS) (S, E): http://www.certifiedmarketingservices.com/, http://www.marketforce.com/, 518.758.6400/1.800.669.9939

Certified Reports, Inc. (CRI) (S, E): http://www.certifiedreports.com/, http://www.marketforce.com/, 518.758.6400/1.800.669.9939

C-Chex—No © or ® on Web site: www.c-chex.com, 585-243-2660

Check Mark, Inc.—No © or ® on Web site (S, E): http://www.checkmarkinc.com/newhome/index-flash.html, 800-866-8836

Checkout (UK) Ltd©: http://www.checkoutuk.co.uk/, 01824-790819

Check-Up Marketing—No © or ® on Web site (E): http://www.checkupmarketing.com/, 800.724.9669

Cirrus Marketing Consultants—No © or ® on Web site: http://www.cirrusmktg.com/, 888-899-7600, 714-899-7600

Clandestine Marketing©: http://www.clandestine.co.za/—No phone number available

Compliance Solutions—No © or ® on Web site: http://www.compliancesolutionsworldwide.com/, 435.232.3888

Confero Mystery Shopping©: http://www.conferoinc.com/, 800-447-3947

Consumer Connection©: http://www.consumerconnection.net/, 604- 740-8182

Consumer Critique, Inc.—No © or ® on Web site: http://www.consumercritique.com/, 503-350-1858

Consumer Impressions, Inc.—No © or ® on Web site: http://consumerimpressions.com/jobopp.htm, 800-747-1838

Consumer Knowledge Analysis (CKA)©: http://www.ckagroup.com/—No phone number available

Consumer Research Group (CRG)®: http://crg2000.com/, 877-889-0602 ext. 222

Corporate Research Group©: http://www.thecrg.com/, 888-215-5147/1-613-596-2910

Corporate Research International™ (S, E): http://www.mysteryshops.com/, 419-422-3196

Corporate Risk Solutions©: http://www.apamysteryshopping.net/, 800-930-1001

Count On Us©: http://www.ucountonus.com/, 856-486-4400

Coyle Hospitality Group©: http://www.coylehospitality.com/, 212.629.2083

Creative Image Associates, Inc.©: http://www.creativeimage.net/, For jobs inquiries, there is no place online. E-mail ciaincorp@aol.com and offer your full name, location and e-mail address and the scheduler for that area will contact you. 888-366-5460, 978-582-7005

Cross Financial Group—No © or ® on Web site: http://crossfinancial.com/, 566-2491/1-402-441-3491

Customer 1st aka Firstpoint Resources© (S, E): http://www.customer-1st.com/, 800-288-7408

Customer Feedback, LLC®: http://www.customerfeedbackllc.com/, 888-333-3225, 425-888-7700

Customer Impact©: http://www.customerimpactinfo.com/, 800.677.2260

Customer Perspectives© (S):
http://www.customerperspectives.com/, 800-277-4677

Customer Service Experts©: http://www.customerserviceexperts.com/, 888-770-7625

Customer Service Perceptions©: www.csperceptions.com—No phone number available. They charge a 2.00 fee to work for them. I do not recommend paying anyone.

Customer Service Profiles©: http://www.csprofiles.com/, 800-841-7954, 402-399-8790

Customerize—No © or ® on Web site: http://www.customerize.com/, 800-330-5948

CV Marketing Research—No © or ® on Web site:
http://www.cv-market.com/, 866-878-7839

Data Quest Investigations, Ltd.©: http://www.dataquestonline.com/, 800-292-9797, 617-437-0030

David Sparks & Associates©: http://www.sparksperry.com/, 864-654-7571

Daymon Worldwide©: http://www.daymon.com/, 203-352-7707

Devon Hills Associates©: http://www.devonhillassociates.com/, 858-456-7800

Diversified Corporate Solutions—No © or ® on Web site:
http://www.divcorp.com/, 800-620-9250

DMS Research—No © or ® on Web site: http://www.dmsresearch.com/, 310-659-8732

Douglas Stafford©: http://www.douglasstafford.com/, 0800 7831913

Draude Marketing©: http://www.draudemarketing.com/, 717-371-5310

DSG Associates©: http://www.dsgstars.com/, 714-835-3020/800-462-8765

Dynamic Advantage©: http://www.dynamic-advantage.com/, 866-870-1251

E-Digital Research©: http://www.edigitalresearch.com/, + 44-(0)1489 772920

Ellis Property management Services—No © or ® on Web site: http://www.epmsonline.com/, 888-988-3767, 972-256-3767

Epinion America—No © or ® on Web site: http://www.epinionamerica.com/, 206-200-9049

Evaluation Systems for Personnel—No © or ® on Web site: http://www.espshop.com/, 713-528-3730

Examine Your Practice©: http://www.examineyourpractice.com/about.php, 866-505-3926

Excel Shopping & Consulting©: http://www.xcelshop.com/, 877-278-7467

Expert Shopping Professionals©: http://expertshoppingpros.com/, (818) 887-2855

Extra Eyes Nationwide, Inc.—No © or ® on Web site: http://www.extraeyes.net/, (916) 480-9724

Feedback Plus, Inc.® (S) (E): http://www.gofeedback.com/, 800-882-7467, 800-816-5050

Field Facts Worldwide—No © or ® on Web site: http://www.fieldfacts.com/, + 44 207 908 6600, 847-419-1278, France, Germany and the United Kingdom only

Focus on Service—No © or ® on Web site: http://www.focusonservice.com/, 888-276-8612

Focus Plus Service Auditors©: Australia, http://www.focusplus.net.au/, 1300 766 545

Franchise Compliance, Inc.©: http://www.franchisecompliance.com/, 435-258-2588

Freeman Group Service Solutions©: http://www.freemangroupsolutions.com/, 972-479-1345

Frontline Shoppers Inc.©: http://www.frontlineshoppers.com/index.htm, 780-448-1654

FSA Automotive Ltd.©: http://www.fsa-automotive.co.uk/OurSolutions/tabid/55/Default.aspx, 01275 876794

Full Scope Mystery Shopping—No © or ® on Web site: http://www.fullscopemysteryshopping.com/—No phone number available

Game Film® Consultants©: http://www.gamefilmconsultants.com/, 866-334-3456

Gapbuster© (S): https://www.xec.gapbuster.com/index.htm, 770-781-3181

GFK-Cybershop (S, E): http://www.cybershoppersonline.com/, 212-240-5300, 800-813-2313

Global Compliance Services©: http://www.pktnshop.com/, 800-553-9807

Goodwin and Associates Hospitality Services LLC© (S): http://www.mysteryshopperprogram.com/, 866-978-3791, 603-223-0303

Graymark Security Group©: http://www.graymarksecurity.com/, 800-881-3242, 954-581-5575

Greet America, Inc.—No © or ® on Web site: http://www.greetamerica.com/, 469-727-0450

Guest Check©: http://www.theguestcheck.com/, 303-991-6173

Guest Perspective Inc.©: http://guestperspective.com/, 888-349 2030

Guest Reflections© SM: http://guestreflections.com/, 888-722-6723

Harland Clarke©:
http://www.harlandeducation.com/mysteryshop.html, 800-291-6117

Harris Teeter: http://www.sassieshop.com/2harristeeter/index.norm.php,
800-296-6699

Hilli Dunlap Enterprises, Inc.—No © or ® on Web site (S):
http://www.dunlapenterprises.com/, 818-760-7688

Hindsight©: http://www.hndsight.com/, 239-849-2210

Hotel Shopping Network©: http://hotelshoppingnetwork.com/, 888-357-
2879, 719-485-7467

ICC Decision Services, Inc.©: http://www.iccds.com/, 800-631-1617,
800.444.1717

ICU Associates, Inc.©: http://www.icuassociates.com/, 877-574-6682

Imaginus, Inc.©: http://www.imaginusinc.com/, 716-688-6500

IMyst™: http://www.imyst.com/, 734-786-8468

Informa Research Services©: http://www.informars.com, 800-848-0218

Infotel©: http://www.infotelinc.com/: 800-876-1110

The Insight Group International©: http://www.theinsightgroupintl.com/,
562-694-3250

Inside Hospitality, LLC©: http://www.inside-hospitality.com/, 888-260-0380

Instant Reply©: http://www.mysteryshopservices.com/—No phone number available

Instant Replays, Inc.—No © or ® on Web site:
http://www.instant-replays.net/, 888-460-SHOP, 919-861-4541

Insula Research©: http://www.insularesearch.com/, 800-975-6234

Integrity Audit Group, Inc.—No © or ® on Web site:
http://www.integrityauditgroup.com/, 800-513-1080

IntelliShop™: http://insite.intelli-shop.com/index.norm.php, 877-894-6349, 419-872-5103

International Service Check©:
http://www.internationalservicecheck.com/, + 49 89 54 55 82 28

Ipsos Loyalty©: http://www.ipsosloyalty.com/, 888.210.7425

i-SPY hospitality audit services, L.L.C.©: http://www.ispy4u.net/, 215.779. 0529

I-Spy Mystery Shoppers—No © or ® on Web site:
http://www.ispymysteryshoppers.com/default.aspx, 402-502-0579

ITS Incognito©: http://www.itsincognito.com/, 0870 746 5672

Jancyn—No © or ® on Web site: http://www.jancyn.com/, 408-267-2600

Jean-Paul & Associates Consultancy©:
http://jeanpaulconsult.com/mystery_shopping.html,
info@jeanpaulconsult.com—No phone number available

Jellybean Services/JBS©: http://www.work4jbs.com/—No phone number available

Jireh Scheduling and Research (All rights reserved):
http://contact-jireh.com/default.aspx, 800-656-3044

J.C. & Associates LLC.—No © or ® on Web site:
http://www.jcandassociates.com/, 719-264-6402

J.M. Ridgeway Company©: http://www.jmridgway.com/, 800-367-7434

JKS Inc.©: http://www.jks-inc.com/home.html, 512-452-0200

Ken-Rich Retail Group©: http://www.ken-rich.com/, 360-756-1403

Keystone Marketing—No © or ® on Web site:
http://www.keystone2000.com/, 949-472-6700

Kinesis-CEM©; http://kinesis-cem.com/, 206-285-2900

LeBlanc & Associates©: http://www.mleblanc.com/, 760-438-1152, 800-838-1779

Legacy Group©: http://www.legacygmr.com/Home_Page.html, 936-444-8524, 832-928-1180

Liberty Research Services LLC©:
http://www.libertyresearchservices.com/, 215-658-0900

Locksley Group Ltd.—No web site, LGLGROUP@aol.com, 800-845-8674

Loss Prevention Associates, Inc.©:
http://www.lpassociates.com/mystreyShoppingComp.html, 714-593-2323

LRA Worldwide, Inc.©, http://www.lraworldwide.com/, 215-957-1999

Management Consultant Group, LLC©:
http://www.managementconsultantgroup.com/—No phone number listed

Maritz Research—Virtuoso© (S): http://www.virtuoso.maritzresearch.com/, 800-782-4299

Market Force© ™ (S, E): http://www.marketforce.com/, 800-669-9939, 770-441-5366

Market Trends Pacific, Inc.—No © found on Web site:
http://www.markettrendspacific.com/, 808-532-0733

Market Viewpoint©: http://www.marketviewpoint.com/, 610-942-7030

Marketing Endeavors, L.L.C—No © or ® on Web site:
http://www.marketingendeavors.biz/, 866-445-9117

Marketing Systems Unlimited, Corp.—No © or ® on Web site:
http://www.msushoppers.com/new_web/index.htm, 800-732-3213

MarketWise Consulting Group, Inc.©: http://www.marketwi.com/, 920-735-4970

Mar's Surveys©: http://www.marsresearch.com/, 954-771-7725

Mystery Shopping Company List

Mass Connections®: www.massconnections.com, 562-365-0200

Measure Consumer Perspectives©: http://www.measurecp.com, 502-499-1139

Melinda Brody and Company©: http://www.melindabrody.com/, 407-294-7614

Mercantile Systems & Surveys©: http://www.mercsystems.com/, 888-222-8301

Merchandise Concepts—No © or ® on Web site:
http://www.merchandiseconcepts.com, States they do mystery shopping, but no sign up page, 636-922-2695

The Mershimer Group, Inc.: 800-723-1150, Partnered with Service Sleuth©, 800-723-1150—U.S., 011 91 98440 42067-India/Asia

Michelson & Associates, Inc©: http://www.michelson.com/, 770-642-2223

Mintel International Group, Ltd.©: http://researchconsultancy.mintel.com/, http://www.services.mintel.com/, 312-932-0400, + 44 (0) 20 7606 4533

Mosaic Info Force—No © or ® on Web site:
http://www.mosaic-infoforce.com/, 800-723-6245, 312-726-1221

Mventix™ (S, E): Market Intelligence Dept.,
http://www.mventix.com, 888-455-2341 x106

Mystery Guest, Inc.©: http://www.mysteryguestinc.com/, 800-777-3882

Mystery Review—No © or ® on Web site: Netherlands,
http://www.mystery-review.com/, + 31 294 45 45 11

Mystery Shoppers—No © or ® on Web site:
http://www.mystery-shoppers.com/, 800-424-0871, 865-450-8841

Mysteryshoppeer.com.au Pty Limited©:
http://www.mysteryshopper.com.au/, 5.00 Application fee—No phone number available

Mystery Shopping Canada, Inc.©:
http://www.mysteryshoppingcanada.com/, 800-752-1295

Mystery Shoppers Ltd.—No © or ® on Web site,
http://www.mystery-shoppers.co.uk/, 01409 255025

Mystery Shop Inc.®: http://www.mysteryshopinc.com/, 866-334-3456

Mystery Shopper Pros, LLC.—No © or ® on Web site:
http://www.mysteryshopperpros.com/, 973-347-1572

Mystique Shopper™: http://www.mystiqueshopper.com/, 813-322-3228

National Investigation Bureau, Inc.©:
http://www.nationalinvestigation.com/, 800-486-1011

Nationwide Services Group, Inc.—No © or ® on Web site:
http://nationwidesg.com/pages/1/index.htm, 800-914-7467

National Shopping Service (NSS)©:
http://www.nssmysteryshoppers.com/, 800-800-2704

National Shopping Service Network LLC.©:
http://www.mysteryshopper.net/, 800-642-2856

National-In-Store (NIS)©: http://www.nis-online.com/index.asp, 800-269-9556

Nationwide Integrity Services Inc—No © or ® on Web site:
http://www.nationwideintegrity.com/, 800-914-7467

New Image Marketing Ltd.©: http://www.nimltd.com/, 239-275-9979

Northwest Loss Prevention Consultants (NWLPC)©:
http://www.nwlpc.com/, 425-271-0312

Nsite Inc.©: http://www.nsiteinc.com/, 888-904-1444, 952-404-1444

Omega Market Research©: http://www.omegamr.com/, 787-704-0917

Opinions Limited LTD.©: http://www.opinionsltd.com/, 440-893-0300

Pacific Research Group©: http://www.pacificresearchgroup.com/, 800-755-8055

PanResearch©: Based in Ireland, http://www.panresearch.ie/, 01-2993800, 00-353-1-2993800

Pat Henry Group LLC©: http://www.thepathenrygroup.com/, 800-229-5260, 216-531-9562

Peak Techniques, Inc.™: http://www.peaktechniques.com/, 770-513-1253

Perfectly Frank, Inc.©: http://www.perfectlyfrankinc.com/, 646-330-5092

Performance Edge—No © on Web site: http://www.pedge.com/, 800-356-9145

PerformaLogics©: http://www.performalogics.com/, 888-855-7467

Perception Strategies©: http://www.perstrat.com/, 877-546-0970

Person to Person Quality©: https://www.adiconsulting.com/ppqsecure/, Certificate error, but safe to proceed, http://www.adiconsulting.com/persontoperson.htm (C), Marc W. Ciagne, 703-836-1517 ext. 102

Phantom Shoppers, LLC©: http://www.phantom-shoppers.com/, 561-350-3420

Pinkerton Compliance Services©: www.pinkertoncompliance.com, 732-842-1518

Premier Services©: http://www.premierservice.ca/, "Due to the over-whelming number of shoppers, we communicate exclusively through E-mail.", info@premierservice.ca, 514-685-1200 In Montreal

800-452-5150

Présence- France—No © or ® on Web site: http://www.presence.fr/, + 33 (0)1.42.33.24.24, + 33 (0)3.20.91.33.33

Professional Review (PROS)©:
http://tinyurl.com/4ttzer (http://www.pinnaclefinancialstrategies.com/products/pros/mystery_shoppers.html), 866-737-1235, 713-868-3333

Profit Strategies and Solutions Inc.—No © or ® on Web site:
http://www.restaurantprofits.com/, 503-449-0356, To apply e-mail:
profitstrategies@aol.com

Promotion Network, Inc.©: http://www.promotionnetworkinc.com/, 708-361-8747

ProSource Evaluation Services™: http://www.evaluation-services.com/, 800-634-4513, 404-806-5569

PulseBack©: http://www.pulseback.com/, 802-362-0900

Quality Assessments Mystery Shoppers©: http://www.qams.com/, 800-580-2500

Quality Assurance Consulting (QACi)—No © or ® on Web site:
http://www.qaci.net/, 866-722-7467

Quality Eye®: http://www.qualityeye.com/, London based, 0870 300 0931

Quality Marketing—No © or ® on Web site:
http://www.quality-marketing.com/, 800-726-0081-CA, 800-933-0081-KS, 800-580-3367-TX, 800-355-4756-FL

Quality Service Inspections (QSI)©: http://www.qsispecialists.com/, 702-891-0550

Quality Service Control©: http://www.qualityservicecontrol.com/, 415-699-8253

Quality Shopper—No © or ® on Web site, http://www.qualityshopper.org—No phone number available

QualityWorks Associates—No © or ® on Web site:
http://www.qualityworks.com/, 888-606-5034, 617-782-0888

Quest for Best—No © on Web site (S): http://www.questforbest.com/, 800-263-5202

Quinn Marketing©: http://www.quinnmc.com/, 800-570-4497

Reality Check Mystery Shoppers©: http://www.rcmysteryshopper.com/, 800-550-4469

Reflections—No © or ® on Web site:
http://prod.koios.com/mri/themes/reflections/site_home.mru?thm = 2,
503-928-6028

Regal Hospitality Group©: http://www.regalhospitalitygroup.com/, 813-854-1855

Remington Evaluations (All rights reserved):
http://www.remysteryshops.com/index.html, 866-485-6491

Rentrak Mystery Shopping©, https://ms.rentrak.com/, 800-929-5656

Research Services Group©, http://www.researchservicesgroup.com/, 404-351-7854

Restaurant Cops©: http://www.restaurant-cops.com/,
http://www.restaurantmysteryshoppers.com/, 210-373-5770

Restaurant Evaluators©: http://www.restaurantevaluators.com/, 773-525-5157

Retail Eyes©: http://www.retaileyes.com, 310-796-0080

RetailTrack—No © or ® on Web site: http://www.retailtrack.com/, 800-576-6860

Richey International©: http://www.richeyint.com/#, 301-656-6622

Rickie Kruh Research©: http://www.rkrmg.com/, 703-298-2381, 561-626-1220

Ritter & Associates©: http://www.ritterandassociates.com/, 877-284-9785, 419-535-5757

Roe Smithson & Asociados Ltda:
http://tinyurl.com/odsujq (http://www.marketresearchlatinamerica.com/
2008/09/12/mystery-shopping/), 56 2-266 9683, 56 7-478 9903

Rocky Mountain Merchandising—No © or ® on Web site:
http://www.rockymm.com/, 801-274-0220.

Sales Quality Group©: http://www.salesqualitygroup.com/index.htm, 480-
967-7500

Satisfaction Services®: http://www.satisfactionservicesinc.com, 800-564-
6574, Sign up for free, no need to pay to be a rated shopper.

Schlesinger Associates—No © on Web site:
http://www.schlesingerassociates.com/index.html, 732-906-1122

Second To None, Inc.©: http://www.second-to-none.com/, 734-302-8400

Secret Shopper Company©: http://www.secretshoppercompany.com/,
877-770-8585, 678-989-2290

Secret Shopping Services—No © or ® on Web site:
http://www.secretshoppingservices.com/, 253-770-0393

SecretShopper.com®: http://www.secretshopper.com/, 763-525-1460

Sensors Quality Management Inc. (SQM)©:
http://www.sqm.ca/NewSQMsi.nsf/indexflash?OpenPage, 416-444-
4491

Sensus Research aka Concerto Research—No © or ® on Web site:
http://www.sensusresearch.com, 866-878-7839

The Sentry Marketing Group, LLC©: http://www.sentrymarketing.com,
214-295-2615

Service Alliance©: http://www.servicealllianceinc.com/, 800-485-2219,
303-696-2147

Service Check©: http://www.servicecheck.com, 877-388-0216

Service Evaluation Concepts (SEC)©: http://www.serviceevaluation.com/, 516-714-0323

Service Excellence Group Inc.—No © on Web site: http://www.serviceexcellencegroup.com/, 800-888-9189, 314-878-9189

Service Impressions—No © on Web site: http://www.serviceimpressions.com/, 916-683-9895

Service Intelligence© (S, E): https://www.experienceexchange.com, 403-261-5000

Service Performance Group Inc.—No © or ® on Web site: http://www.spgweb.com/, 866 567-8300

Service Quality Department: This site and its contents, (c) 1990-2008 Customer, Loyalty Builders, Inc., All Rights Reserved.: http://www.service-quality.com/, 800-432-2456, 925-798-0896, Note: There is no need to pay Platinum or Gold shopper fees to work for this company.

Service Research Corporation (SRC)©: http://serviceresearch.com/, 877-825-5772, 402-434-5000

Service Savvy©: http://www.servicesavvy.com/, 763-208-6229

Service Sleuths—No © on Web site: http://www.howardservices.com/homess.html, 800-723-1150

Service With Style©: http://www.servicewithstyle.com/, 877-OBSERVE, 813-661-1775

ServiceCheck©: http://www.servicecheck.com/, 877-388-0216

ServiceProbe©: http://www.pwgroup.com/sprobe/, 423-517-0554

Service Quality Solutions aka Buckalew Hospitality: E-mail to be added to shopper database, DaveBuckalew@aol.com, 407-810-6596

ServiceSense©: http://www.servicesense.com/, 800-465-1182

Service Traq©: http://www.servicetrac.com, 800-951-6606

SG Marketing©: http://www.sgmarketing.com/,
http://www.marketforce.com/, 303-402-6920

Shadow Agency©: http://www.theshadowagency.com/, 877-874-2369,
817-281-1100

Shoppers Critique International LLC© (S):
http://www.shopperscritique.com/, 800-633-6194, 407-834-3337

Shoppers Inc.©: http://www.shopperjobs.com/, 800-259-8551

Shopper's View—No © or ® on Web site: http://www.shoppersview.com/,
800-264-5677

Shopping by Mystery—No © or ® on Web site:
http://www.shoppingbymystery.com/services.html, 208-559-1550

Signature, Inc.©: http://www.legendary.net/, 800-398-0518, 614-766-5101

Sinclair Service Assessments (SSA) ©: http://www.ssanet.com/, 800-600-
3871, 210-979-6000

Sipe and Associates LTD.—No © or ® on Web site:
http://www.sipeandassociates.com/pages/1/index.htm, 520-744-5927

Six Star Solutions©: http://www.sixstarsolutions.com/Home.html, 877-
274-2213, 801-274-2213

Skilcheck Services©: http://www.skilcheck.com/, 209-333-4555

SNEAK PEAKms—No © or ® on Web site:
http://spbon.com/HomePage.asp, 319-351-0211

Solomon Group®: http://www.thesolomongroup.com/, 800-505-7952

Southwest Mystery Shoppers©: http://www.mysteryshoppers.com/,
Apply for free:
http://www.mysteryshoppers.com/index_files/EmploymentApplication.
htm, 915-440-4882

Sparks'Perry Research©: http://www.sparksperry.com, 800-849-7467 (Shopper), 864-654-7571

Speedback©: http://www.speedback.com/, 510-837-5955

Spies in Disguise—No © or ® on Web site: http://spiesindisguise.com/, 866-557-9648

Spysee Mystery Shopping©: Australia, http://www.spyseebiz.com.au/, 0408 412 614

Startex Marketing Services®: http://www.startexmarketing.com/newapp/, LaHore, Pakistan, 92-21-4265611

Statopex©: http://www.statopex.com/en/, 450-682-7150

Store Insight—No © or ® on Web site:
http://www.sassieshop.com/2storeinsite/index.norm.php—No Phone number available

Strategic Reflections Inc.—No © or ® on Web site:
http://www.strategicreflections.com, 866-518-6508

Support Financial Resources, Inc.©: http://www.serviceexperiences.com/, 800-444-5465, 937-434-5700

Sutter Marketing, Inc.—No © or ® on Web site: http://suttermarketing.com/, 847-358-3100

Taylor Research©: http://www.taylorresearch.com/, 800-922-1545, 619-299-1414

Tell Us About Us Inc.—No © or ® on Web site:
http://www.tellusaboutus.com/, 877-301-5469, 204-453-4757

Tenox aka In Touch Shoppers©: http://www.intouchshoppers.com/, 800-461-2873

The Emmerich Group, Inc.©: http://emmerichfinancial.com/, mysteryshopping@EmmerichGroup.com, 800-236-5885

The SEER Group, LLC©: https://www.theseergroup.com/, https://www.theseergroup.com/Become_a_Shopper.html, 302-478-6369

TES/RapidCheck©: http://www.tnsmi-tes.com/profile.htm, 800-767-2291

Testshopper.com—No © or ® on Web site: http://testshopper.com/, 410-381-9292

Texas Shoppers Network, Inc.™: http://www.texasshoppersnetwork.com/, 877-465-6656, 713-984-7631

TNS Intersearch©: Mystery Clicks, http://www.mysteryclicks.com/, 800-767-2291

Total Research Solutions, Inc.©: http://www.totalresearchsolutions.com/, 619-923-2978

TrendSource© (S, E): http://www.trendsource.com/, 619-718-7467

Varga Research & Associates, Inc.—No © or ® on Web site: http://www.vargaresearch.com/, 407-472-5851

Video Eyes©: http://www.videoeyes.net/, 866-645-5588

ViewPoint Consumer Reporting—No © or ® on Web site: http://www.viewpointcr.com/index.htm, E-mail for more information: jwustman@viewpointcr.com, 760-943-0528

Wal-Mart©: http://www.walmart.com/cservice/ca_research.gsp?NavMode = 8—No phone number listed

Zellman Group©: http://www.zellmangroup.com/, 516-625-0006

Scheduling companies and other places to register to find jobs:

BLD Scheduling Services—No © or ® on Web site: http://bldschedulers.com/, 650-235-8383

Client Smart©: https://shoppers.clientsmart.com/—No phone number available

Coast To Coast Scheduling Services—No © or ® on Web site: http://ctcss.com/, 562-943-0646

KSS International©: http://www.kernscheduling.com/, Varies by scheduler. Write your schedulers number here:

Mystery Shopping Solutions©: http://www.mystshopsol.com/—No phone number available

Quality Scheduling Group, LLC©: http://www.qualityscheduling.com/, 732-567-5064

Other contact information you may need: MSPA-www.mysteryshop.org, 972-406-1104

About the Author

PamInCa is a Gold Certified mystery shopper. She has been mystery shopping for eight years and decided to write a book to help people who want to learn all of the ins and outs of this fantastic business. She has completed over 16,000 mystery shops from apartments to casinos. For the last four years she has taken jobs that she would not normally take for the sole purpose of research for this book. She has not paid for groceries, gas, dining out, office supplies or even hotels for the last eight years.

About the Author

Recommended Happy About® Books

Purchase these books at Happy About
http://www.happyabout.info
or at other online and physical bookstores.

42 Rules for Working Moms

This book is a compilation of funny practical advice on how to survive as a "working mom". Laura Lowell brought together a diverse group of working moms: different cultures, industries, ages, relationships and perspectives.

Paperback: $19.95
eBook (pdf): $14.95

Lessons About Life Momma Never Taught Us

This book describes the lessons and insights the three authors derived from their experiences and problems with boys.

Paperback: $14.95
eBook (pdf): $14.95

CPSIA information can be obtained at www.ICGtesting.com
Printed in the USA
LVOW05s1515141213

365169LV00001B/12/P